# Fun with Literacy

### 100s of Activities, Exercises and Tips for the Classroom & Therapy (Birth-Preschool)

## Karen Thatcher, Ed.D., CCC-SLP

Copyright© 2017

Published by:
PESI Publishing & Media
PESI, Inc.
3839 White Ave.
Eau Claire, WI  54703

Cover Design: Amy Rubenzer
Editing: Amy Farrar
Layout: Amy Rubenzer, Jennifer Wilson-Gaetz

Proudly printed in the United States of America
ISBN: 9781683730590

PESI Publishing & Media
www.pesipublishing.com

# Acknowlegments

The completion of this book would not be a reality without the many children and families that became excited when literacy became a possibility in their lives. Many parents believed their child would not or could not experience the excitement that books bring to our lives. The delight that these parents exhibited when their child participated in the literacy experience only fueled my passion to continue with this resource. I would also like to thank the many early interventionists that were open to my ideas about literacy and incorporated them into their therapy sessions.

In addition, I want to thank my daughters Danielle and Abigail who from the day they were born, were my biggest supporters. They have made me want to be a better mother, teacher, and woman.

Finally, to my grandson Tyler. Mimi loves you and am so excited that you are a lover of books. Literacy will be the special bond we will always share.

# About the Author

**Karen Thatcher, EdD, CCC-SLP**, has over 20 years of early intervention experience, working on multidisciplinary teams to facilitate the language, social-emotional, cognitive, gross and fine motor, and feeding skills of children birth to preschool. She has also presented extensively to multidisciplinary audiences on how to incorporate literacy into therapy and a child's daily routine.

Dr. Thatcher is an Associate Professor at Samford University in the Department of Communication Sciences and Disorders in Birmingham, Alabama. She teaches both graduate and undergraduate courses in language development, language disorders, cognitive-communicative disorders and diagnostics.

# Table of Contents

# Introduction

As parents, educators, therapists, and administrators, we all realize the critical importance of literacy in our everyday lives. Being literate is something that many of us take for granted; we may not fully understand what being literate means or what becoming literate involves.

What is literacy? The conventional definition is being able to read, write, and understand the world of language and text. This definition also includes the ability to use and understand oral language and is considered the "historical" viewpoint.

However, there is also another facet of literacy that must be considered, particularly for children with disabilities who receive early intervention and preschool services, called "personal literacy" (McVicker and Thatcher, 2005). The definition of personal literacy is attempting to read, write, and understand at a personal developmental level. The term personal literacy suggests that all children can benefit from being involved in oral language and print-related activities.

Literacy begins developing well before children enter formal schooling. Evidence-based research shows that the developmental period between birth and age three is crucial to developing not only oral language but the foundation of literacy. This research has led to an increased awareness and focus on the environmental supports for emergent literacy and the role it plays in the development of formal literacy (Dickinson and McCabe, 2001). Emergent literacy can be widely defined as the skills that form the foundation before a child learns to read and write. These include book handling, understanding that books contain stories (which stay the same every time they are read), understanding that the print on the pages corresponds with the pictures on them, and being able to grasp the concept that stories have a beginning, middle, and end.

In fact, examine the following:

- The home literacy environment significantly affects both oral language and literacy development and in fact, highly correlates to later academic success (Scheffner Hammer, Farkas, Maczuga, 2010).

- The age at which parents and caregivers begin reading to their child is highly correlated to the development and quality of the child's language development (Duursma, 2014).

- Literacy and oral language skills in kindergarten and first grade predict school achievement and even the completion of high school (Froiland, Powell, Diamond, Son, 2013).

- "Failing to give children literacy experiences until they are school-age can severely limit the reading and writing levels they ultimately attain" (IRA and NAEYC, 1998, p. 30).

- It has been suggested that intervention implemented after children are three years old, especially for children in low-income households, may have limited impact on later cognitive or developmental skills due to the cumulative effects of experiences during the first three years of life (Hart and Risley, 1995).

Historically, many parents and teachers viewed children with special needs as incapable of learning, using, or needing literacy, resulting in limited access to literacy opportunities. In fact, the more severe the disability, the more typical was this reaction. However, this viewpoint has changed significantly. Goldstein (2011) notes, "Today's challenge is to apply new and emerging literacy to all children, and in particular to provide a foundation for literacy in early childhood for children with and at risk for disabilities." Many children with or at risk for disabilities may also exhibit an increased risk for literacy deficits. Consider the following:

- Children with disabilities (speech and language, vision, hearing, physical/motor, multiple disabilities, cognitive) are at significant risk for developing reading deficits (McDonnel, Hawken, Johnston, Kidder, Lynes, McDonnell, 2014).

- Approximately 50% of preschool children with language delays develop a reading disability (Catts, 1993).

- Koppenhaver, Pierce, and Yoder (1995) indicate, "Research suggests that in cases where literacy is incorporated into daily routines and interventions, many individuals with severe disabilities make good progress in learning to read and write" (p. 7).

- Johnston, McDonnell, and Hawken (2008) note that, "In summary enhancing the engagement of children with disabilities in emergent literacy activities may require the use of specific strategies for adapting instruction" (p. 214).

Research has also shown that the literacy experiences of children with disabilities (most notably those with severe and multiple disabilities) tend to be much different than those of children without disabilities (Goldstein, 2011). Specifically, children with disabilities may have less access to literacy experiences (book handling, shared-book reading, observing literacy use within the environment, etc.). Of particular concern is that these children require more exposure to a literacy rich environment and opportunities in order to begin developing a possible foundation for literacy. Understanding the literacy needs and limitations of these children provides a critical platform for early intervention providers. Many teachers and therapists now acknowledge the importance of literacy for children with special needs, but feel inadequately trained on how to instruct these children in reading and writing.

It should be noted that research indicates that children with special needs do respond favorably to literacy, even from birth to three years of age. A study conducted by Thatcher and McVicker (2005) documented numerous positive responses of children with disabilities to literacy opportunities, including:

**Literacy Behaviors
Children with Special Needs
(Birth to Three Years Old)**

88% enjoy pictures in books

64% become excited when read to

52% pretend to read

44% name some pictures

18% ask simple questions

81% have easy access to books

13% repeat rhymes and stories

58% enjoy repeated readings

44% enjoy various types of books

12% try to fill in familiar words

71% enjoy sitting close

# What This Means to the Early Intervention Provider

Early intervention service providers must utilize and adhere to the guidelines of developmentally appropriate practices. All areas of infant and toddler development are interrelated, including gross and fine motor, oral and written language, social, and cognitive skills. Specifically, development in one area influences and is influenced by development in other areas (NAEYC, 2009). In fact, research has shown a positive correlation between the physical movement of a child and cognitive development (Kirk, Vizcarra, Looney, and Kirk, 2014). Ironically, this is not a new theory. Tomporowski, Davis, Miller, and Naglieri (2008) note that, "Since the time of the ancient Greeks, there has been an implicit belief that physical activity is linked to intellectual abilities" (p. 111).

Evidence-based research dictates that if we are to make more meaningful connections across these developmental areas, we must make intervention more effective. A developmentally appropriate curriculum must provide for different aspects of a child's development, including cognitive, physical, social, linguistic, emotional, and aesthetic. In addition, funding for early intervention programs is becoming more difficult to justify in many states. By utilizing a developmentally appropriate individualized program for each child, we can ensure that what we do in early intervention is working and is cost effective. Finally, linking literacy to therapy is *fun,* for the child and the therapist.

# Roles the Early Intervention Provider Can Take in Literacy

Implications for the early interventionist may include several key components:

- Educating parents and other providers on the link between oral language and literacy.
- Educating ourselves on how to incorporate literacy into oral language, gross and fine motor skills, and social activities.
- Providing literacy models for parents and caregivers.
- Encouraging and assisting parents and other providers in accessing books and activities.
- Educating parents to advocate for their child's literacy development after leaving early intervention.
- Participating in emergent literacy research.
- Identifying children at risk for not developing literacy.

We all play a vital role in the development of the infants and children that we serve. As providers, we not only affect a child's current development, we also have the ability to shape a child's future academic and social success. Incorporating literacy into therapy goals allows us as providers and parents to meet the developmental needs, abilities, and interests of children with special needs. As we provide services to children with special needs, we must understand and advocate for best literacy practices for these children (see below).

## Best Literacy Practices for Children With Special Needs

**Literacy must be:**

- Viewed as being possible
- Accessible
- Convenient
- Not based on conventional assumptions
- Inclusive
- Multi-sensory
- Developmentally appropriate
- Innovative
- Repetitive
- Social and interactive
- Visually stimulating
- Offered in a nurturing, positive environment
- Personal!

# Literacy into Therapy!

## How to Use This Resource

First of all, let's have a serious discussion about the **secret** of literacy into therapy. Of course adapting your therapy to include literacy has to be hard, doesn't it? No! This resource offers providers a *Literacy Prompt,* which for many will be very familiar rhymes, *Mother Goose* verses, and songs we knew as kids. If you don't know a song, make up your own tempo, notes, and rhythm. Even if you do know it, you can still make up new verses, rhythms, and notes.

Following each *Literacy Prompt* are *Literacy and Therapy Activities,* which are easy, practical, and inexpensive to incorporate into any discipline's therapy session. In fact, many of the activities do not require the therapist or teacher to make any additional materials. Of course, you can be as creative as you like, including literacy/therapy activities of your own.

---

**All templates and posters can be downloaded
and printed off from www.pesi.com/Thatcher**

---

## The Secret of Literacy into Therapy

- Have fun with it!
- See literacy in everything.
- Think outside of the box - look at things differently.
- Always be on the lookout for a literacy experience.
- Find your resources.
- Make it easy and practical.
- Make it cheap.

Also included in this resource is a *Literacy into Therapy Action Plan* to be utilized by all disciplines and parents. It can be used weekly or monthly to document the *Literacy Prompts* that are used and the activities that are utilized by each discipline. This ensures a continuity of services and promotes literacy education for parents. An example of a plan is included on the following page.

**EXAMPLE**

# Literacy into Therapy Plan

**Literacy Prompt:** *The Itsy Bitsy Spider*

| | |
|---|---|
| **Parent** | Took a walk looking for spiders and other bugs! During bath time put in plastic bugs and we counted them and caught them with a butterfly net |
| **PT** | After we sang the Itsy Bitsy Spider song we crawled on the floor like a spider – Plastic bugs were placed throughout the living room and we hunted for them walking backwards! |
| **OT** | We used the connect the dot spider to make a spider picture and then we colored it - then we sprinkled glitter on the spider to make him shiny! |
| **ST** | After singing the literacy prompt we went outside for a walk and looked for different bugs. We talked about ants, butterflies, grasshoppers, spiders, and lady bugs. After our walk we read a book about a sad spider and why he was so sad. |
| **DT/Teacher** | We sang the song Itsy Bitsy Spider and talked about what "itsy bitsy" means. What are some other things that are "itsy bitsy"? We also talked about what a "water spout" is and where we would find one. |

# Literacy into Therapy Plan

**Literacy Prompt:**_____

| | |
|---|---|
| **Parent** | |
| **PT** | |
| **OT** | |
| **ST** | |
| **DT/Teacher** | |

# The Three Little Kittens

The three little kittens, they lost their mittens,
and they began to cry,
Oh Mother dear, we sadly fear,
See here, our mittens we have lost.
What! Lost your mittens,
you naughty kittens!
Then you shall have no pie.
Mee-ow, Mee-ow, Mee-ow.
No, you shall have no pie.
The three little kittens,
They found their mittens,
And they began to cry,
Oh Mother dear, see here, see here,
Our mittens we have found.
Put on your mittens, you silly kittens,
And you shall have some pie.
Purr-r, purr-r, purr-r,

Oh, let us have some pie.
The three little kittens put on their mittens
And soon ate up the pie,
Oh Mother dear, we greatly fear
That we have soiled our mittens.
What! Soiled your mittens,
you naughty kittens!
Then they began to cry,
Mee-ow, Mee-ow, Mee—ow,
Then they began to sigh.
The three little kittens
they washed their mittens
And hung them out to dry,
Oh Mother dear, do you not hear
That we have washed our mittens.
What! Washed your mittens,
you are good kittens.

1. Sing the song aloud with the child/children.

2. Read the poem or sing the song aloud. Using the poster, have a child help you point to each word using his/her finger, a pointer, or a flashlight as you read.

3. Read the poem a second time and have the children participate by voicing and motioning along with you as much as possible. Introduce hand gestures/finger plays to engage the children.

## Suggestions for Hand Motions/Finger Plays:

- Hold up three fingers when you say "three."
- Sign "kitten," by bringing your index finger and thumb tips together on each side of the mouth and move hands away from the face in a quick double movement (as if stroking the whiskers of a kitten).
- Hold your hands in front of you when you say "mittens."
- Move your fists up to eyes and rub as if crying when you say "cry."
- Shake your head side to side when you say "no."
- Hold your hands out to the side, palms up, and shrug your shoulders when you say "lost."

# Mitten Maker
**ACTIVITY 1**

## Color/Decorate Paper Mittens

## MATERIALS NEEDED:

- Mitten template (pages 14-15)
- Scissors
- Glue
- Markers or crayons
- Decorative items:
    Small paper dots from hole puncher in a variety of colors
    Feathers
    Beans
    Colored sand
    Small bits of paper
    Other small objects

## DIRECTIONS/OPTIONS:

- Copy or print the mitten template for children to color/decorate.
- Have the children decorate the mitten by coloring and/or gluing different decorative items to the paper mitten.

## GROSS MOTOR:

- **Stair Climbing:** Locate a wall with stairs leading up and down from it or create stairs using benches/stools. Tape the picture of the mitten to the wall. Work on climbing up and down the stairs, placing one foot on each step. Have the child color the mitten for 30 seconds or place decoration on the mitten when he or she reaches the top. Have the child climb down the steps to switch color of crayon or collect another decoration.

- **Core/Proximal Shoulder Strengthening:** The child will be activating/working his or her core muscles/shoulders while coloring against the wall.

## FINE MOTOR:

- **Visual-Motor/Pre-Handwriting Skills:** Instruct the child to color the picture using vertical, horizontal, or circular strokes/scribbles. Choose a direction that will present an appropriate challenge.

- **Grasping Skills (Pincer):** Have child use a pincer grasp to pick up small items and to attach them to the mitten.
- **Scissor Skills:** Direct the child to snip small pieces of colored paper to use as decoration. If the child is able to make consecutive snips to cut through paper, have him or her cut the mitten out after it is colored/decorated.

## ORAL LANGUAGE:

- **Expressive Language/Speech:** Encourage the child to imitate words from the poem. Begin with simple one-syllable words (pie, no, some, us), move to two-syllable words (kitten, mitten, naughty, mother). Use the pictures on the poster to discuss the meaning of the words you choose to practice.
  - If the child is not yet able to produce words, encourage sound play of "mmm," "p," and "k." Begin by having the child imitate these sounds in isolation. Talk about the features of each sound:
    - Feel "mmm" on your nose. Your tongue is resting and your lips are touching.
    - Hear and feel the quiet burst of air from your mouth with the "p" sound. Your tongue is resting and your lips close then open slightly.
    - Hear and feel a quiet burst of air from your mouth with the "k" sound. The back of your tongue touches the back of your mouth/throat. Your lips rest open.
  - Once mastered, practice adding the vowels from the poem, such as: mee-ow, my, pie, kit(tens); encourage the child to imitate the consonant-vowel combination (do not worry about every sound in the word).
- **Rhythm, Prosody, and Voice:** Have the child voice along with you while you read/sing the poem. Encourage the child to attempt the sounds/words you have practiced as you read.
- **Phonological Awareness:** Talk about rhyming: Rhyming words sound alike, but differ by the first sound. Eventually have the child identify the rhyming word from a list of three. Finally, tell the child to come up with his/her own rhyming word (true word or nonsense word):
  - Pie-Cry
    Which word rhymes with pie: eat, play, my
    Say another word that rhymes with pie:_____
  - Dear-Fear-Here
    Which word rhymes with dear: pier, dig, sun
    Say another word that rhymes with dear:_____
  - Kittens-Mittens
    Which word rhymes with kitten: paper, smitten, table
    Say another word that rhymes with kitten:_____

- **Receptive Language/Vocabulary/Basic Concepts:** Compare and contrast the child's mitten with your own, or another mitten. Talk about the concepts of "same" and "different" in regards to size, color, shape, and details/decorations.

# WRITTEN LANGUAGE:

- **Pre-Literacy Skills:** Using the included poster, read/sing the poem with the child while helping him/her follow along with the text from left to right with his/her finger, a flashlight, or a pointer.

# SOCIAL/PRAGMATIC:

- **Sharing Information:** Have the child share with others how he or she is decorating the mitten. Model basic concept vocabulary words including color, texture, shape. Encourage more descriptive vocabulary including (red, sparkly, sticky, etc.) and ask the child questions about what he/she is doing/using to make the mitten, to encourage expressive use of descriptive words.

- **Generalizing/Relating to Experiences:** Encourage the child to talk about mittens he/she has at home, or in which books/movies he/she has seen mittens. Talk about when and why he or she would wear mittens.

- **Turn-Taking Skills:** Take turns with the child, each time sharing one detail about the mitten/s.

# COGNITIVE SKILLS:

- **Patterning:** Help the child make a pattern using the materials. Begin an "AB" pattern with the decorative items. Ask or help the child continue the pattern you begin, or create his/her own pattern while decorating the mitten. Once the "AB" pattern is mastered, move onto "ABB" or "ABC" patterns.

  | | |
  |---|---|
  | AB: | ABABABA_ |
  | ABB: | ABBABBAB_ |
  | ABC: | ABCABCAB_ |

- **Following Commands:** Ask the child to follow simple commands such as, "Draw a big circle" or "Color the thumb of the mitten green."

- **Counting:** Help the child count the number of (colors/stamps/stickers/etc.) and encourage them to vocalize or count with you.

# SENSORY:

- **Tactile Exploration:** Use small items of varied textures (e.g. sand, grains, rice, and feathers) as decoration.

# Mittens

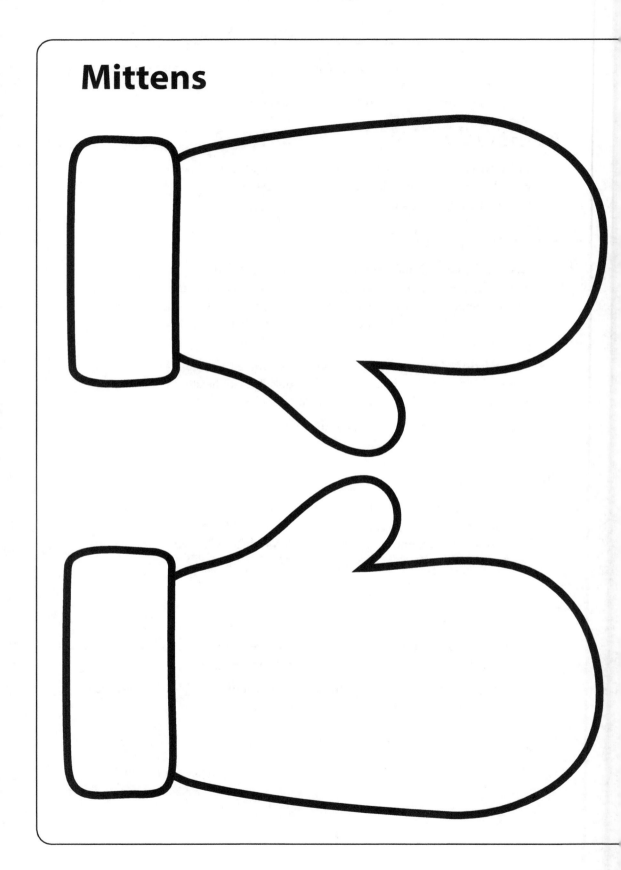

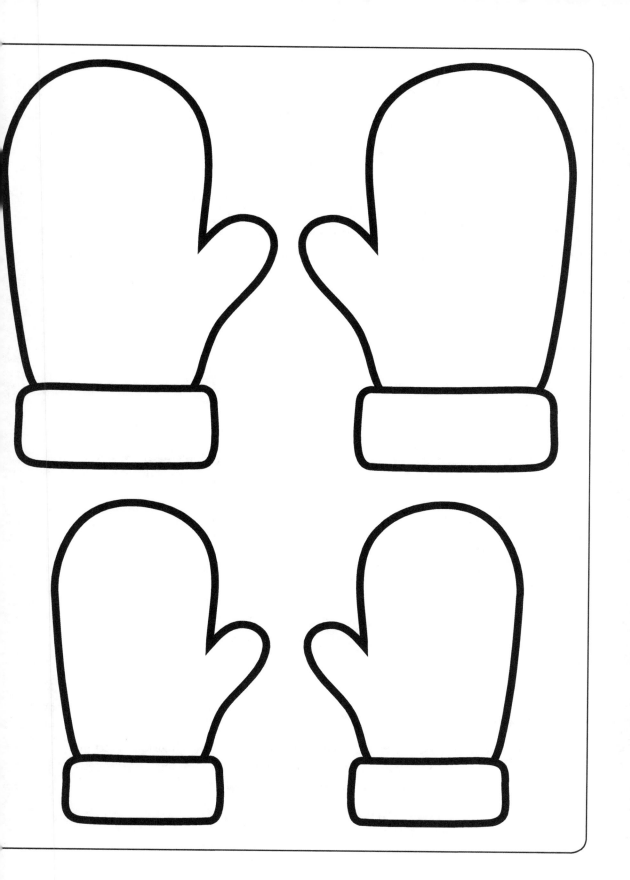

# ACTIVITY 2 — Mitten Hunt

## MATERIALS NEEDED:

Mittens—Choose one of the following options:

- The paper mittens decorated by the child/children in the previous "Mitten Maker" activity
- Use copied/printed Mitten Template from pages 14-15 to cut out mittens
- Real mittens

## DIRECTIONS:

- Hide mittens around the room.
- Determine and mark the "starting point."
- Have the child stand/sit/kneel on the "starting point."
- Direct the child to locate one mitten and then return to the starting point.
- Continue until the child locates all of the hidden mittens.

## GROSS MOTOR:

- **Locomotion:** Direct the child to perform a movement or action each time he/she moves from the starting point to locate a mitten:

| | |
|---|---|
| Walk | Hop on one foot |
| Walk backward | Hop on two feet |
| Walk sideways | Gallop |
| Run | Crab walk |
| Skip | Wheelbarrow |

## FINE MOTOR:

- **Fine Motor Dexterity/Hand Strengthening:** After the child locates a mitten and returns to the starting point, have him or her perform one of the following options based on the materials/equipment available to you:

- Attach the mitten to a clothespin suspended from a string or taped/attached to a wall.
- Attach the mitten to a bulletin board using a pushpin *(with close supervision)*.
- Attach the mitten to a dry erase board, magnetic board, or metal furniture using a small magnet.

## ORAL LANGUAGE:

- **Vocabulary/Basic Concepts/Auditory Comprehension/Expressive Language:** Focus on the basic concepts of position and placement (on, under, beside, behind) to hide and/or find the mitten.
  - Give the child a simple clue or direction to find the hidden mitten (e.g., "It's *beside* the desk" or "It's *under* something you sit on.")
  - Ask the child a simple question to lead them to the hidden mitten (e.g., Hide the mitten in the sink and then ask, "Where do you wash your hands?" to help the child find the mitten).
  - Have the child hide the mitten. Model/help them give you hints or directions to find the mitten.

## WRITTEN LANGUAGE:

- **Pre-Literacy Skills:** Talk about the sound "mmm" at the beginning of the word "mitten," and describe how the letter "M" makes this sound. Have the child practice drawing an "M" in the air with his/her index finger before going to find the mitten, and after returning to the "starting point."

## SOCIAL/PRAGMATIC:

- **Asking Questions to Obtain Information:** Model "yes/no" questions, and encourage the child to imitate or spontaneously ask "Is it" questions to find the mitten: "Is it on the floor?"; "Is it in something?"; "Is it in the trash can?"). You may want to draw cues or write the questions and answers to give the child a visual way to remember the questions he/she has asked.

## COGNITIVE SKILLS:

- **Visual Closure:** Position objects on top of the hidden mittens, partially obstructing them from the child's view as he or she looks for them.
- **Figure Ground:** Position the mittens among other objects, requiring the child to differentiate the mitten from the background.

## SENSORY:

- **Tactile Exploration:** Use plastic tubs or boxes to make sensory baths. Fill them with things like: sand, rice, beans, textured balls, beads, and ribbon.

  Place the hidden mittens in the sensory baths. Position the mittens on top of the bath's contents for a light challenge or partially submerge them in the contents to make the task more challenging.

  Instruct the child to remove the mittens from the sensory baths.

# ACTIVITY 3 — "I'm Missing a Mitten!"

## MATERIALS NEEDED:

- Mitten Template or five to ten pairs of real mittens
- Equipment for an obstacle course:

  Mat(s)                     Hula hoop
  Cone(s)                    Rocker board
  Bench                      Seesaw
  Chair                      Balance beam
  Scooter                    Foam roll and/or wedge
  Trampoline                 Heavy blanket
  Tunnel

## DIRECTIONS:

- Set up the obstacle course.
- Prepare five mitten pairs by printing/copying the mitten template on pages 14-15 and cutting the mittens out. Add up to ten mitten pairs as needed to provide an appropriate challenge for each child. You can use real mittens in place of the paper mittens.
- Place one of each mitten pair at the start of the obstacle course and one at the end of the obstacle course.
- Show the child one mitten and cue him or her to find the matching mitten at the other end of the obstacle course. The child should move through the course before locating the matching mitten.

  If this presents too great a challenge, allow the child to bring the first mitten with him or her through the course as a visual cue.
- Have the child return the mitten to the start of the course to pair the mittens together.

## GROSS MOTOR:

- **Locomotion/Strengthening:** Instruct the children to move through an obstacle course. Some options for obstacles are:
  - Benches to step up on and jump or step off of
  - Walk on a balance beam moving forward, side to side or backward

- Jump into/out of a hula hoop
- Jump over a roll or small object
- Crawl through a tunnel
- Crawl under a mat or weighted blanket
- Bounce on a mini trampoline
- Walk over an unstable surface (e.g. rocker board, seesaw).
- Weave in and out of obstacles (e.g. cones, large blocks, cups).
- Use a scooter board
    - Work in prone position using arms to propel
    - Work in sitting position using feet to propel
- Crawl under chairs
- Climb/step/jump on or off of stacked mats

## FINE MOTOR:

- **Dressing:** Have the child put the mittens on and take them off if you use real mittens.

- **Manipulation/Dexterity:** Have the child use a paper clip or small pinch clip to attach the two mittens in the pair together.

## ORAL LANGUAGE:

- **Receptive/Expressive Language/Speech:** Answer questions and learn new information about kittens at the beginning and end of the obstacle course:

    **Talk about the features of kittens:** Do kittens have hair or fur? How many legs does a kitten have? What are kitten's "hands and feet" called?

    **Talk about the lives of kittens:** Where do you see kittens? What do they eat? What sounds do kittens make?
    Practice saying the word "kitten" (or sound "k").

## WRITTEN LANGUAGE:

- **Pre-Literacy Skills:** Talk about the sound "mmm" at the beginning of the word "mitten," and describe how the letter "M" makes this sound. Have the child practice drawing an "M" in the air with his/her index finger before going to find the mitten, and after returning to the "starting point."

- **Pre-Literacy Skills:** Write a letter on a mitten and hide it. Provide the child or children with a copy of the letter and have them try and find that particular mitten.

## SOCIAL/PRAGMATIC:

- **Generalization/Problem-Solving:** Talk about a time when you lost something at home: How did you find it? Who helped you find it? What can you do with your things to keep them from getting lost?

- **Team Work:** Have the children work in teams to find the missing mittens. Talk about how working as a team can be faster and easier than trying to do something alone.

## COGNITIVE SKILLS:

- **Visual Memory:** Show the child a mitten at the start of the course and cue them to remember what it looks like so he or she can find the matching mitten at the end of the obstacle course.

## SENSORY:

- **Tactile Exploration:** Set up an obstacle that provides a sensory experience.
  Have the child step through a bean or rice bath.
  Have the child search for an object submerged in a bean or rice bath.

# Kitten Pie

## MATERIALS NEEDED:

- Play-Doh®

- Plastic knife

- Rolling pin, plastic bottle, cup, etc.

- Items to decorate the pie:

  | | |
  |---|---|
  | Macaroni pasta | Red Hots |
  | Beans | Raisins |
  | Cereal (Fruit Loops, etc.) | Pretzel sticks |
  | Chocolate chips | Gum drops |

## DIRECTIONS:

- Have the child/children roll out the Play-Doh or help them as needed.

- Press the mouth of a plastic cup into the Play-Doh and have them trace/cut out around the mouth of the plastic cup to make a round circle, or the "pie crust."

- Allow the child/children to finish the pie using the additional ingredients – make sure they understand that they CANNOT eat the pie because the "crust" is not real.

## GROSS MOTOR:

- Have the child complete the "pie" while standing on a rocker board/wobble board or sit on a t-stool/therapy ball.

- **Core/Shoulder Strengthening:** Cue the child to stand up or sit up tall as he or she prepares the "pie." The child will be activating/working his core muscles while rolling the "dough" and adding ingredients.

## FINE MOTOR:

- Allow the child to soften, roll, and manipulate the Play-Doh with fingers. Have him "roll" the pie dough.

- Show the child how to pinch around the "pie crust."

- **Pincer Grasp:** Have the child use pincer grip to retrieve and place the decorative items for the pie.

## ORAL LANGUAGE:

- **Vocabulary:** Bring in and talk about the different utensils and terms used when baking and cooking (spatula, spoon, rolling pin, pie pan, mixer, oven, boil, etc.). What can be used if you don't have these items?

- **Description:** Talk aloud to the child as you both make your "pie." Describe what you are doing (I'm rolling the dough; I'm pinching the edges of the crust, etc.). Encourage the child to describe what he is doing as well.

- Talk about what kittens eat. Would kittens eat pie? What kind of pie does the child like/dislike?

- **Phonemic Awareness:** Have the child roll the Play-Doh with the rhythm of the song.

## WRITTEN LANGUAGE:

- Have the child make letters in the Play-Doh when it is rolled out or make letters out of Play-Doh.

## SOCIAL/PRAGMATIC:

- **Sharing:** Talk about how pies, cakes, pizza, etc. are cut into several pieces so that many people can share the food item. Talk about how to divide pieces so that it is fair to all.

## COGNITIVE:

- **Measuring:** Show how a pie, pizza, cake, etc. can be cut into different sizes to get more or less pieces. Talk about concepts such as more, less, big/bigger/biggest, etc.

- **Colors:** Have the child name the colors used for his pie. What color crust did he or she use, what color items did she or he use to decorate it?

## SENSORY:

- **Tactile Exploration:** Allow the child to manipulate the Play-Doh, rolling it into a ball, snake, etc.

- Place small items (beans, marbles, etc.) in the Play-Doh and have the child pick them out with his/her fingers.

# ACTIVITY 5

# Let's Make Some Kitten Chow

## MATERIALS NEEDED:

- Print the template on page 26 to list out the ingredients you are using.
- A large bowl
- Small bowls—one for each ingredient
- Scoops or measuring cups
- Spoons
- Two to three of the following to make the "Kitten Chow":
  Goldfish® crackers
  Cereal (e.g. Cheerios®, Grape Nuts®, Granola)
  Small pretzels
  Small crackers
  Other snack foods

## DIRECTIONS:

- Place each of the ingredients into separate small bowls.
- Have the child systematically combine the ingredients in the large bowl.
- Have the child stir the ingredients together using a spoon.
- Have the child use a clean cup to scoop out a serving for him or herself.

## GROSS MOTOR:

- **Balance:** Have the child stand on a rocker board/wobble board or sit on a t-stool/therapy ball as he or she makes the "kitten chow."
- **Core/Shoulder Strengthening:** Cue the child to stand or sit up tall as he or she prepares the "kitten chow." The child will be activating/working his or her core muscles/shoulders while stirring the ingredients.

## FINE MOTOR:

- **Forearm Rotation:** Instruct the child to use scoops or measuring cups to scoop the ingredients out of the small bowls and dump them into the large bowl.

- **Self-feeding:** Have the child use a spoon to transfer the ingredients from the small bowls to the large bowl. This technique will also address forearm rotation and fine motor dexterity.

- **Pincer Grasp:** As the child eats the snack, cue him or her to pick up one piece at a time using a pincer grasp. If the child does not eat the snack, have him or her release one piece at a time into a bowl to "feed the kitten."

## Oral Language:

- **Vocabulary:** Discuss the ingredients used in the "kitten chow" and how most foods we eat have ingredients. The ingredients for each food will be different depending on what is being made. Talk about the items used to make the "kitten chow," such as the scoop, spoon, bowls, etc.

- **Concepts:** Talk about concepts such as in/out, stirring, pouring, mixing, measuring, etc.

- **Following Directions:** Provide verbal instructions for making the "kitten chow." You may need to provide a visual model in conjunction with the verbal instructions.

- Talk about what other animals eat. What do humans eat? What are the child's favorite foods, foods he dislikes, etc.?

- **Phonemic Awareness:** Stir the mixture to the beat and rhythm of the song.

## Written Language:

- Have the child cross off the steps of the recipe as he adds it to the mixture.

- Allow the child to look at the containers of ingredients. Talk about what information we can find on the labels, how we use labels, etc.

## Social/Pragmatic:

- **Turn Taking:** Allow each child to add an ingredient and stir it into the mixture.

- **Sharing:** Have the child or children take some of the "kitten chow" and put it into sandwich baggies to share with others.

## Cognitive Skills:

- **Counting:** Have the child count the individual ingredients as he or she adds them to the mixture.

- **Memory:** After the "kitten chow" is done, have the child list all the items he or she put into the chow mix. Provide visual cues as needed.

## Sensory:

- **Tactile Exploration:** Have the child wash his or her hands and then mix the items together in the large bowl using his or her bare hands.

# Kitten Chow

**Ingredients:**

_____   _____
_____   _____
_____   _____
_____   _____
_____   _____
_____   _____

**Directions:**

_____
_____
_____
_____
_____
_____
_____
_____
_____
_____
_____
_____
_____
_____
_____

# ACTIVITY 6

# Copy Cat
## (Birth to Three Years of Age)

## MATERIALS NEEDED:

- Mirror
- Objects to manipulate:
    Blanket
    Socks
    Ball
    Rattle
    Stuffed animal
    Finger food

## DIRECTIONS:

- You can use the mirror if you want, but if not, that's okay too.
- Make different facial expressions, body movements, gestures, noises, etc. and encourage the child to copy you. The suggested movements for this song would be great to use too!

## GROSS MOTOR:

- Model any gross motor skill appropriate for the age and skill level of the child.
- Sing the song and practice walking like a cat, walk soft/loud, slink, pounce, etc.

## FINE MOTOR:

- Model those fine motor skills appropriate for the age and skill level of the child.
- Allow the child to wash him or herself—first like a cat does, then using a washrag.

## ORAL LANGUAGE:

- **Practice making different animal noises.** Use the stuffed animals, if available, to use with the different noises. Practice purring.
- Talk about new words in the song such as purring, naughty, silly, etc.

- **Same and Different:** Talk about different animals and what they look like. How are cats and dogs the same or different? Compare obviously different animals such as a fish/worm, bird/cow, etc. How do other animals get along with each other?
- **Phonemic Awareness:** Stomp or clap the rhythm of the song as you sing it. Use the mirror if available.

## WRITTEN LANGUAGE:

- **Pre-Literacy:** Look at books with lots of animals. Talk about the pictures in the book, encourage the child to point to animals as he/she sees them, make the noises of the animals as he/she sees them, etc.

## SOCIAL/PRAGMATIC:

- Talk about how the cat washes herself and how we wash ourselves. Use a washrag with different temperatures of water, etc. Talk about how important it is to be clean.
- **Emotions:** Talk about emotions such as sad, happy, mad, etc. How do we know the kittens were sad/happy? What did they do when they were sad/happy?

## COGNITIVE:

- **Counting:** Count with the child the number of animals seen in the book when looking through it.
- Have the child maintain eye contact during the song and while being a "copy cat."

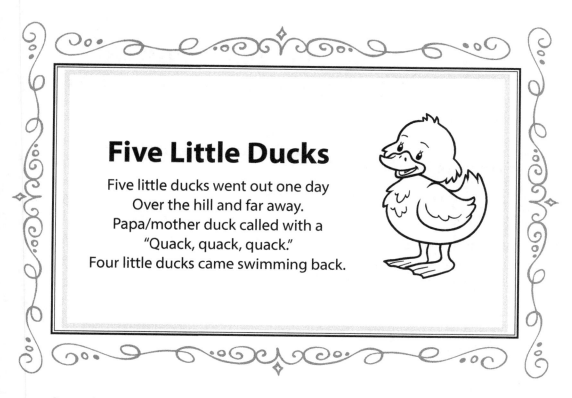

# Five Little Ducks

Five little ducks went out one day
Over the hill and far away.
Papa/mother duck called with a
"Quack, quack, quack."
Four little ducks came swimming back.

Repeat, losing one more duck each time until you are left with one duck. Have papa/mother duck call and end with "five little ducks came swimming back."

1. Sing the song aloud with the child/children.
2. Read the poem or sing the song aloud. Using the poster, have a child help you point to each word using his/her finger, a pointer, or a flashlight as you read.
3. Read the poem/song again and have the child/children participate by voicing and motioning along with you as much as possible. Introduce hand gestures/finger plays to engage the children.

## Suggestions for Hand Motions/Finger Plays:

- Hold up five, four, three, etc. fingers when you say the number.
- Sign "duck" by using the forefinger and middle finger to tap the thumb in front of the mouth to mimic the movement of a duck's bill.
- Use your hands in a sweeping motion to mimic the ducks going over the hill.
- Use your hands to cup your mouth as if calling for someone far away.
- Move arms as if swimming.

# Make and Take Duck
## Color/Paint and Decorate Paper Ducks

## MATERIALS NEEDED:

- Duck template (page 35)
- Glue/tape
- Decorative items
  Ribbon
  Cereal (Fruit Loops® are fun!)
  Buttons
  Small, colorful pieces of paper
  Pictures from a magazine
  Small pom-poms

- Scissors
- Markers, crayons, or paint
- Paintbrush or feather

## DIRECTIONS/OPTIONS:

- Copy or print the duck template for children to cut, color/paint and decorate.
- Have the children decorate the duck by coloring, painting (use the feather!), or gluing different items to the paper duck.

## GROSS MOTOR:

- **Locomotion:** Have pictures of ducks pasted in different areas of therapy area. Show the child different ways to "move" towards the ducks.

| | |
|---|---|
| Walking | Walk sideways |
| Waddling | Skip |
| Swimming | Run |
| Hopping | Rolling |
| Jumping | Crab walk |

# Fine Motor:

- **Pincer Grasp:** Have the child paint using the feather.
- **Scissors Skills:** Have the child snip small pieces of magazine pages to use as decoration. If the child is able to make consecutive snips to cut through paper, have him or her cut the duck out after it is colored/decorated.

# Oral Language:

- **Expressive Language/Speech:** Sing the song using other animals. Talk about where the other animals live and how they move and act out the movements.
  - If the child is not yet able to produce words, encourage them to make the sounds that each animal makes.
  - Play with sounds and talk about features of the sounds "d," "mmm," and "k."
    - Feel "d" with your tongue behind your top teeth.
    - Feel "mmm" on your nose. Your tongue is resting and your lips are touching.
    - Hear and feel a quiet burst of air from your mouth with the "k" sound. The back of your tongue touches the back of your mouth/throat. Your lips rest open.
- **Rhythm, Prosody, and Voice:** Have the child sing along with you while you sing. Overemphasize the vocal inflection and use hand movements to keep rhythm with the song and show when the inflection goes up or down.
- **Phonological Awareness: Talk About the Sounds in the Song.** Have the child "quack" every time he or she hears the target sound in the song. Sing the song with different animals and have the child make that animal sound when they hear the target sound.
  - Start with sounds in the beginning of the word (listen for the "d", as in duck).
  - Progress to sounds at the end of words (listen for the "k" like in quack).
  - Finally target sounds in the middle of words (listen for "d" like in waddling).
- **Receptive Language/Vocabulary/Basic Concepts:** Cut out more ducks in different sizes, colors, and textured paper. Talk about how they are the same and different. Have the child put them in order of largest to smallest or organize them by color.

# Written Language:

- **Pre-Literacy Skills:** Fold paper together to make a book. Have the child "write" his or her own story about ducks. You can either do the writing for the child or the child can pretend to write his own words. Encourage him or her to draw pictures with the story. Have him or her retell the story with you and model skills such as starting from the left of the page and moving to the right, starting at the top, and having a beginning, middle, and end.

## SOCIAL/PRAGMATIC:

- **Sharing Information:** Have the child tell you or others about how he or she is decorating the duck. Provide many different decorating options and model the basic vocabulary words including color, texture, and shape. Model social skills by asking questions, such as asking for "more" of something or asking the child if you can have some of his or her glue.

- **Generalizing/Relating to Experiences:** Verbally model a time when you saw ducks and other animals. Encourage the child to tell about a time they saw animals, maybe at the zoo or the lake.

- **Turn-Taking Skills:** Take turns using the scissors, glue, or other decorations with the child. Talk about how nice it is to share with others.

## COGNITIVE SKILLS:

- **Following Commands:** Play "Mother Duck Says" in a similar fashion to the "Simon Says" game. Have the child follow commands such as "Waddle like a duck" or "Find the blue duck."

- **Counting:** Have enough ducks cut from paper to sing the song. Have the child remove a duck from the poster or wall every time a duck does not come back. The child can then put all the ducks back at the end of the song when they all come swimming back!

## SENSORY:

- **Tactile Exploration:** Use small items of varied textures (e.g. sand, grains, rice, and feathers) as decoration.

# ACTIVITY 2

# Ducks on Parade

## MATERIALS NEEDED:

Ducks (Choose one or combine the following options):

- The paper ducks decorated by the child/children in the previous "Make and Take Duck" activity
- Copy and make new ducks from Duck Template on page 35
- Use rubber ducks
- Use Peeps® ducks and chicks

## DIRECTIONS:

- Place the ducks in different places around the room.
- Have the child retrieve each duck and bring it to the parade route.
- After the child finds all the ducks, have him or her line them up as if they are in a parade.
- Have the child "lead" the parade around the room.

## GROSS MOTOR:

- **Locomotion:** Have the child use target gross motor skills to move along the parade route. Make it an obstacle course by placing common objects in the parade route for the child to move around, over, under, etc.
  - Move the parade outside.

## ORAL LANGUAGE:

- **Vocabulary/Basic Concepts:**
  - Ask the child to name other animals that could be part of the parade.
  - Have the child line up the ducks on the parade route from smallest to largest.
- **Expressive Language:**
  - Have the child tell the ducks where they are going as they march in the parade or describe what he or she is seeing along the parade route.
  - Talk about other ways people move or travel (by car, train, plane, or boat).

- **Phonological Awareness:** Sing the song and have the child march along the parade route. When you stop singing, the child will stop marching (or anytime the child hears the target sound or word he or she stops marching).

## WRITTEN LANGUAGE:

- **Pre-Literacy Skills:** Have the child make his or her own map of the parade route or you can draw landmarks of the route as the child tells them to you.

## SOCIAL/PRAGMATIC:

- **Turns:** Take turns being the leader of the parade, deciding the parade route, or deciding the type of locomotion (marching, walking, running, hopping, etc.)

## COGNITIVE SKILLS:

- **Counting:** Using permanent marker, write the numbers 1-10 on the bottom of the rubber ducks and place them in a bucket or tub of water. Let the child pick a duck and then put them in the correct order.

- **Colors:** Using permanent marker, color a small circle on the bottom of the rubber ducks. The child can choose a duck and name the color, or choose ducks with a certain color on them.

- **Visual closure:** Position the ducks where they are partially hidden. Have the child play hide and seek to find the ducks.

## SENSORY:

- **Tactile Exploration:** Place all of the ducks (paper, rubber, Peeps) in a bag and have the child reach in and describe what he or she feels. Have the child reach in and try to grab the targeted texture.

# Duck

<blockquote>
**ACTIVITY**
**3**
</blockquote>

# Digging for **Ducks**, and other Stuff

## MATERIALS NEEDED:

- Empty jar (peanut butter, mayonnaise, etc.)
- Rice, sand, birdseed, sugar, etc.
- Small items to place inside the jar

## DIRECTIONS:

- Take the clean, empty jar and fill it with one of the following: sand, rice, birdseed, Rice Krispies®, etc.
- Place several of the small items in the jar and shake. Items can be small toy animals, buttons, rhyming words, items that start with the same letter, plastic letters, etc.
- Roll the jar in your hands to move the contents and have the child find and name the items they see.

## GROSS MOTOR:

- **Locomotion:** Have the child roll the jar on the floor with their hands and legs straight (bending at the waist).

## FINE MOTOR:

- **Pincer Grasp:** Dump sand, rice, etc. in a bowl with small items and have the child pick them out with his or her fingers.
- **Pre-Handwriting Skills:** Have the child color each item they find on a small piece of paper and stick each one on the outside of the jar.

## ORAL LANGUAGE:

- **Expressive Language/Speech**
  - Encourage the child to name all the items he/she sees/finds in the jar. They can discuss the category (animals, colors, rhyming words, etc.) that each belongs in.
  - Have the child organize the categories before putting them in the jar. The child can describe or discuss why they are in the same category.

<blockquote>
</blockquote>

- The child can describe how big the objects are in real life.
- Play "I Spy" with the items seen in the jar.
- Use items with the child's target speech sounds (the child must say them correctly).
- Use small toy animals and have the child make an animal noise when they see the corresponding animal in the jar.
- **Phonological Awareness:**
  - Place one item in the jar that does not rhyme with the others. Have the child identify which one does not rhyme.
  - Use 3 or 4 categories of items that have the same first letters (items that start with p, m, and k). Have the child say the item he sees in the jar and then identify the first letter.
- **Receptive Language/Vocabulary/Basic Concepts:** Use items the child is not familiar with to increase the new vocabulary. Have the child describe how the items move in the contents.

## WRITTEN LANGUAGE:

- **Pre-Literacy Skills:** Have the child copy or write the name of the category in the jar and tape it on the side of the jar.

## SOCIAL/PRAGMATIC:

- **Turn-Taking:** Take turns finding items in the jar, asking nicely.
- **Generalizing/Relating to Experiences:** Talk about a time when the child was in a crowded place. Practice saying, "Excuse me," etc.
- **Sharing Information:** Have the child describe to the other children what he or she sees in the jar.

## COGNITIVE SKILLS:

- **Patterning:** Have the child put items from the smallest to the largest in the jar and then find them.
- **Counting:** Have the child count items as they put them in the jar. Write down the number and keep looking until he/she finds all the items, tallying each item he or she finds.

## SENSORY:

- **Tactile Exploration:** Dump the contents of the jar in a bowl and have the child find the items with his or her fingers.

# ACTIVITY 4

# Bird Feeder

## MATERIALS NEEDED:

- Toilet paper or paper towel roll
- Bird seed
- Paper plate
- String or Yarn
- Creamy peanut butter
- Plastic knife
- Hole punch

## DIRECTIONS:

- Use the hole punch to place two holes on either side of one end of the roll.
- Use the knife to spread peanut butter over the entire paper towel or toilet paper roll.
- Place bird seed on the paper plate.
- Roll the peanut butter-covered roll in the bird seed, covering the entire roll with bird seed.
- Cut the string and tie it through the holes to make a hanger.
- Place the bird feeder outside where the child can see the birds coming to eat!!

## GROSS MOTOR:

- Have the child complete the activity while sitting or balancing on a therapy ball or t-stool.
- Allow the child to take his or her bird feeder outside and hang it in his or her place of choice. Use a chair, stool, or other appropriate device to hang the feeder high enough.

## FINE MOTOR:

- Allow the child to spread the peanut butter either with the knife or with his or her fingers if appropriate.
- The child can sprinkle the birdseeds over the roll instead of rolling it.
- Have the child stick his or her fingers inside the tube to move it as he or she is rolling it in the birdseed.
- Allow the child to place yarn through the hole and tie if appropriate.

## ORAL LANGUAGE:

- **Vocabulary:** Talk about the different kinds of birds, where they live, what they look like, whether all birds can fly, etc.

- **Description:** Provide pictures of different birds and have the child describe what each one looks like. Has the child ever seen that type of bird, where, etc.

- What do different types of birds eat? Some eat fish, bugs, birdseed, etc.

- Talk about famous birds such as Woody Woodpecker, Big Bird, Chicken Little, Tweety Bird, Mother Goose, the Ugly Duckling, Donald Duck, etc. Where do we see these famous birds?

- **Phonemic Awareness:** As you complete the bird feeder, choose key words in the activity (bird, seed, peanut, butter, plate, eat, etc.). Provide 2-3 more words and have the child identify the word that starts with the same letter. For example, "Listen to 'bird'. It starts with the 'b'" sound (be sure to make the sound of the letter, not the letter's name). Which of these words starts with the same sound? Chicken, big, goose."

## WRITTEN LANGUAGE:

- Have the child look at the container/sack that the birdseed came in. Compare it to other labels. How are they the same/different? What type of information do we find on the birdseed container?

- Have the child make a "restaurant" sign for the bird feeder. For example, "Best seed in town" or something cute or catchy!! Or have them make a menu for the bird feeder!!

## SOCIAL/PRAGMATIC:

- **Manners/Social Skills:** Talk about how we act when we go out to eat in public restaurants, using the menu to order food, the difference between fast food and sit down restaurants, etc.

- **Generalization:** Talk about a time that the child or children went out to eat. What was it like? What types of food did they eat?

## COGNITIVE:

- **Problem-Solving:** Give the child the toilet paper roll and birdseed without covering it with the peanut butter. Why won't the bird seed stick? What can we do to make it stick?

## SENSORY:

- **Tactile Exploration:** Put small items (ball, crayons, chips) in the birdseed and allow the child to find them using his or her hands.

## ACTIVITY 5 — Quackers for You!

### MATERIALS NEEDED:

- Graham crackers
- Plastic knife
- Plastic spoon
- Sealable sandwich bag for each topping
- Paper plate
- Icing (store-bought works great!)
- Two to three of the following to make "quackers":
    Sprinkles (different colors, different types of sprinkles)
    Oreos or other cookies (crush in sealable baggie)
    Chocolate chips
    Crushed dried pineapple
    Crushed nuts
- Recipe template on page 42

### DIRECTIONS:

- Have the child spread the icing on the graham crackers.
- Have the child use a spoon to sprinkle on toppings.
- If you crush the toppings (cookies), have the child crush them with a rolling pin.
- Place "quackers" on a paper plate.

### GROSS MOTOR:

- Have child carry "quackers" on the paper plate like they are carrying a tray, like a restaurant server would.

### FINE MOTOR:

- Have the child use a plastic knife to spread icing on a graham cracker.
- Have the child break crackers into smaller pieces.
- Have the child use his or her thumb and first two fingers to sprinkle toppings.

# ORAL LANGUAGE:

- **Expressive Language:**
  - Have the child give another child or yourself directions on how to make "quackers."
  - Instruct the child to describe what each item tastes like (sweet, smooth, crunchy, etc.)
- **Phonological Awareness:**
  - For each item the child finds, he or she will say three rhyming words.
  - While smashing items or sprinkling items on graham crackers, have the child segment words that match the action they are doing ("sprin-kle").

# WRITTEN LANGUAGE:

- **Pre-Literacy Skills:** Have the child use sprinkles to make letters on the graham crackers.

  Provide directions for making "quackers" written on the template for the child. Have the child cross off each step as he or she completes it.

# COGNITIVE SKILLS:

- **Sequencing:** Have the child explain the next step of making "quackers" before they do it.
- **Visual Memory:** Sprinkle a letter on a graham cracker and then have the child copy you with sprinkles and a cracker.
- **Generalization of Experiences:** The child talks about the time he or she helped someone cook or bake.

# SENSORY:

- **Tactile Exploration:** Have the child feel the differences in the different items sprinkled on graham crackers.
- **Oral Exploration:** Have the child taste different textures of sprinkles and other toppings used on graham crackers.

# Quackers for You

**Ingredients:**

_____  _____

_____  _____

_____  _____

_____  _____

_____  _____

_____  _____

**Directions:**

_____

_____

_____

_____

_____

_____

_____

_____

_____

_____

_____

_____

_____

_____

_____

_____

# Bird Watch
## (Birth – Three Years of Age)

**ACTIVITY 6**

## MATERIALS NEEDED:

- Stuffed animals (lots of birds!!)
- Scissors
- Windows
- Paper towel or toilet paper rolls
- Yarn
- Tape

## DIRECTIONS:

- Place the stuffed animals around the room where the child can see them. Or you can open the windows or take a walk outside.
- Either cut the paper towel roll in half or use two toilet paper rolls, and tape them together to make a pair of "bird watching" binoculars.
- Tape yarn to the binoculars so that they can be worn around the child's neck (if appropriate for the child).
- Look around the room or outside and try to find as many birds or other animals as you can!!

## GROSS MOTOR:

- **Locomotion:** Use appropriate locomotion for the child's skill level or goals. For example, walking while holding the child's hand or crawling.
- **Neck and Head Control:** Place the birds in locations that require the child to look up and move his or her head from side to side.

## FINE MOTOR:

- **Pincer Grasp:** Allow the child to hold the binoculars or assist him/her as needed.
- Place the stuffed animals within reach of the child so that he/she will attempt to grasp them.
- Allow the child to assist in making the binoculars (as appropriate).
- If the child is unable to speak or is too young to speak, have him/her point to the birds and animals he/she sees.

## ORAL LANGUAGE:

- **Following Directions:** Verbally provide cues to help the child locate the birds. For example, "I see a bird sitting on a table. Can you find it?"
- Have the child describe the bird she/he sees. When you find the bird she/he is describing, provide more details such as, "Yes, the bird is blue!"
- **Vocabulary:** Talk about words such as wing, beak, fly, nest, claws, etc.
- **Vocal/prosody:** As you sing the song, use one of the stuffed birds to move in a rhythmic motion, encouraging the child to sing along with you.
- **Phonemic Awareness:** For younger children, hold their hands and clap along with the song as you sing. For older children, they can clap by themselves.

## WRITTEN LANGUAGE:

- **Pre-Literacy:** Read books with lots of birds and animals. Point to the animals and encourage the child to point as he sees the animals.

## SOCIAL/PRAGMATIC:

- **Eye Contact:** Sing the song to and with the child. Make sure to make eye contact and encourage eye contact.
- Talk to the child about how it is okay to look/stare at the animals but how it is not polite to stare at people.

## COGNITIVE:

- **Counting:** Place five birds in front of the child and sing the song. As you sing, take away one bird to follow along with the song. Then count all the birds again when they all come back!!
- **Colors:** Talk with the child about the different colors on the birds and animals.

## SENSORY:

- **Auditory Stimulation:** Take the child outside and listen for birds chirping or other animals (such as dogs barking!!).
- **Tactile Stimulation:** Use the stuffed animals to stroke the child as appropriate. You can also use a feather.

# The Hokey Pokey

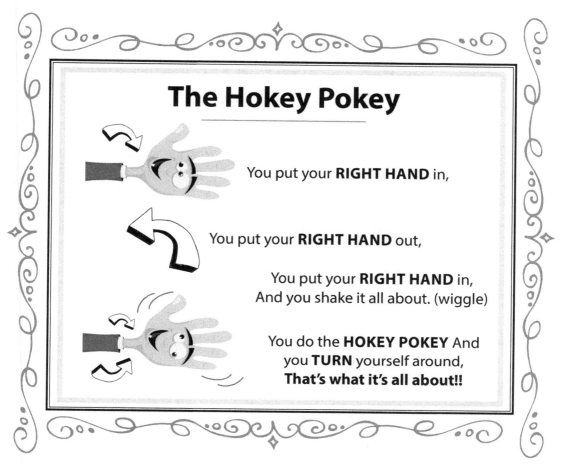

You put your **RIGHT HAND** in,

You put your **RIGHT HAND** out,

You put your **RIGHT HAND** in,
And you shake it all about. (wiggle)

You do the **HOKEY POKEY** And
you **TURN** yourself around,
**That's what it's all about!!**

Continue with other verses that put in other parts of the body and finish up with your entire body.

1. Sing the song aloud with child/children.
2. Read the poem or sing the song aloud. Using the poster, have the child touch each word with a hand, pointer, or ruler as it is sung/said.
3. Sing the song again, encouraging the child or children to sing along. Let them try to sing the parts they know by themselves. Over-exaggerate body movements following the song.

## Suggestions for Hand Motions/Finger Plays:

- Wave hands back and forth in front of you when "doing the Hokey Pokey."
- Shake body parts when you "shake it all about."
- Turn your body around in a circle after doing the "Hokey Pokey."
- Clap hands with words/syllables when saying, "That's what it's all about!"
- Point at the child and instruct the child to point to you every time "you" is sung.
- Modify the Hokey Pokey for children who cannot stand by having other motions they can do from a sitting position. Or include a motion that involves them going from a crouching to a standing position or a sitting to a standing position.

## ACTIVITY 1   "Pin Me"

### MATERIALS NEEDED:

- Body parts: use copied/printed Body Parts templates from pages 48-49 to cut out body parts.
- Body: have the child lie down on a large sheet of paper and draw the outline of his/her body.
- Tape
- Blindfold

### DIRECTIONS:

- Have the child cut and color the body parts.
- If the child can, have him/her cut out the shape of his/her body.
- Tape the body on the wall where the child can completely reach all of it.
- Spin the child around while he/she is wearing the blindfold, stopping her/him in front of the body and facing it.
- Give the child a body part with tape on it and have him try and put the body part in the correct area.

### GROSS MOTOR:

- **Locomotion:** If you don't turn the child around in a circle, have them hop, skip, dance, etc. to the body shape/cut-out.
- **Balance:** Practice "up" and "down" by having the child crouch down low and then stand up, or by having her/him step up onto a stool.

### FINE MOTOR:

- Make extra body parts for the child to color and decorate.
- Have the child trace her/his own hands and feet and cut them out.
- Let the child color the body shape/cut out to look like her/him, with the same color hair, eyes, and color of clothes.

## ORAL LANGUAGE:

- **Vocabulary:** Have the child name all of his/her own body parts before beginning the game.

- **Describing:** Have the child tell what he/she can do with the body part he/she put on. For example, "I can clap my hands, I can run with my feet, etc."

- **Asking Questions:** If the child is blindfolded, have them ask questions to make sure they are in the right area to place a body part. For example, "Am I close to the hands? Do I need to go up?, etc."

- **Auditory Comprehension:** Give the child verbal cues as they try to place the body parts on the silhouette. For example, "move your hand to the left"; "Move your hand up until I say stop", etc.

- **Phonemic Awareness:** For each body part the child puts on, have him/her name words that rhyme with it.

## WRITTEN LANGUAGE:

- **Pre-Literacy Skills:** Have the child trace or copy letters or words of the body parts, just like as he/she did when tracing his/her hands and feet.

## SOCIAL/PRAGMATIC:

- Talk with the child about keeping their "hands to themselves" and respecting "each other's space."

## COGNITIVE:

- **Patterning:** Pattern the body parts on the floor. For example, "hand, hand, foot", "foot, foot, foot, head."

- **Auditory Memory:** Use hands and feet to clap and stomp a beat or rhythm and have the child repeat it. Start simple and move on to more complicated patterns.

## SENSORY:

- **Tactile:** As the child is placing a body part on the silhouette, rub or tap on the child which body part he/she is closest to, placing the body part to help cue placement.

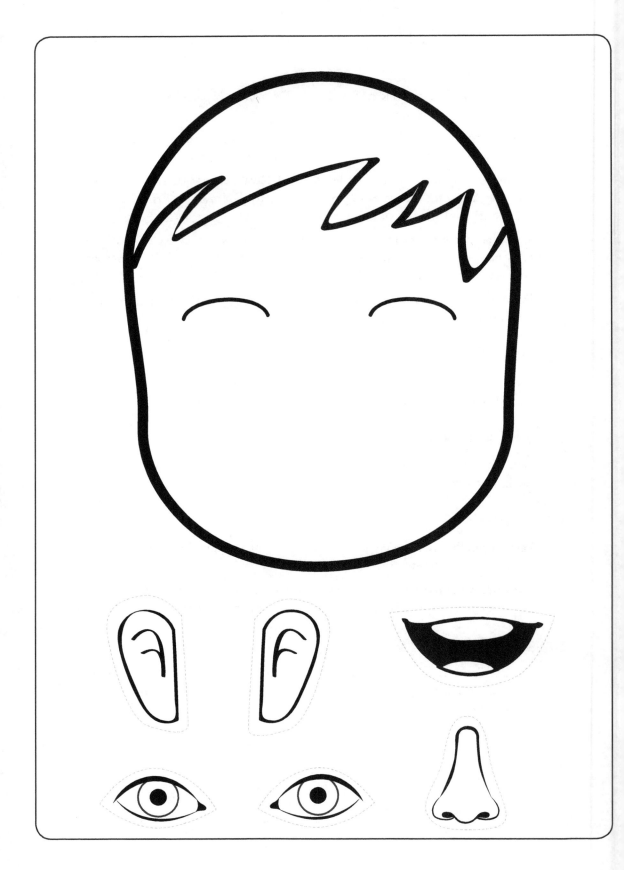

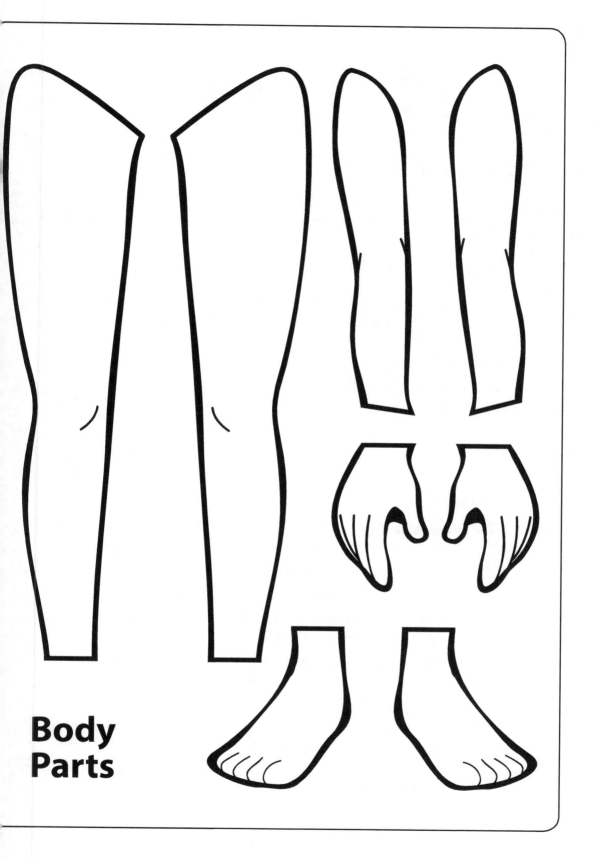

**Body Parts**

# ACTIVITY 2 — Grab Box

## MATERIALS NEEDED:

- Different articles of clothing or accessories
- A big box with a hole in the top so that the child can't see into it, but large enough to pull an item out.

## DIRECTIONS:

- Tell the child to "find something that goes on your foot" and then have the child search through the box only by feeling objects to find the shoe, etc.

## GROSS MOTOR:

- **Locomotion:** After the child identifies an article of clothing, have him/her put it where it belongs. He/she can skip, walk, hop, etc. to where it belongs (for example, coat in closet/cubby).
- **Balance:** Have the child stand on one foot while putting on each article of clothing.

## FINE MOTOR:

- **Daily Living Skills:** The child will put on shoes and tie them, put on a jacket and zip/button it, put on socks, etc.
- The child can fold the articles of clothing.
- **Pincer Grasp:** The child can grab articles of clothing from the box.
- **Visual Closure/Memory:** Hide the clothing items among different clothes and have the child find the one that was hidden.
- Have the child make hand puppets out of old socks. He/she can draw a face on the sock and then use his/her hand to make it talk. Great for oral language too!!

## ORAL LANGUAGE:

- **Expressive Language:** Have the child tell which body part an article of clothing belongs on.
- Have the child tell what each article of clothing does. For example, shoes protect our feet and coats keep us warm.

- Have the child describe the article of clothing by the way it feels when he/she is finding it in the box, before he can see it.

- Have the child describe his/her favorite outfit to wear.

- **Vocabulary:** The child can name the article of clothing, its color, etc.

- **Auditory Comprehension:** Describe an article of clothing to the child and have him/her find it in the box with his/her hand, before he/she can see the clothing.

- **Phonemic Awareness:** Have the child identify articles of clothing that start with same letter. For example, "socks," "shoes," and "shirt."

## WRITTEN LANGUAGE:

- Use catalogs or store ads to locate similar items of clothing.

- Have the child make price tags for how much each item of clothing is worth.

## SOCIAL/PRAGMATIC:

- Have the child talk about a time when he/she did not have an article of clothing that they needed. For example, not having a coat on a cool day.

- Discuss with the child the differences in clothing choices made by different people and cultures.

## COGNITION:

- Have the child line up items in order, from biggest to smallest.

- When looking at the store ads or catalog, discuss which items cost more, adding the prices together.

## SENSORY:

- **Tactile Exploration:** Have the child use only touch to find items without seeing them in the box. If the child is having difficulty finding an object, you can give clues to what it feels like. For example, "A shoe has laces, so you will feel strings hanging from the shoe."

# Shake it All About

## MATERIALS:

- Different containers with lids.
- Different filler items of various sizes, weights, etc. For example, rice, marbles, buttons, paper, water, popcorn kernels, etc.

## DIRECTIONS:

- Fill different containers with the different fillers so that each container will make a different sound when shaken.
- Have the child shake all of the different containers to hear the different sounds each item(s) make.

## GROSS MOTOR:

- Have the child shake the container making large movements. The child may also jump up and down, hop, or skip to listen to the sounds the objects make as they shake the containers.
- Have the child use the shaker container during the Hokey Pokey.

## FINE MOTOR:

**Pincer Grasp:**

- Have the child fill an empty container (for example, dropping rice or marbles into a bottle).
- Have the child use another container to scoop and pour filler items into the shaker container.
- Make the containers different sizes with different types of lids. Have the child open and close the lids on the containers.

## ORAL LANGUAGE:

- **Basic Concepts:** Have the child describe how each shaker sounds when it is shaken. Include concepts such as soft, loud, etc.
- **Expressive Language:** Have the child choose the filler item and describe how he/she thinks it will sound before shaking it. After shaking the container, discuss

again whether he/she was right, how it was different, what made it sound that way, etc.

- **Phonemic Awareness:** Use the shaker to count the beat while doing the Hokey Pokey. Use the shaker to count the beat to other songs and rhymes.
- **Phonemic Awareness:** Have the child identify the first letter of filler items as they are shaking it and then find words that rhyme. For example, "'B' for 'beans'— beans rhyme with means, deems, seems, etc."

## WRITTEN LANGUAGE:

- **Pre-Literacy Skills:** Use the filler items to make letters on the floor or table. For example, popcorn, beans, buttons.

## SOCIAL/PRAGMATIC:

- **Turn Taking:** Do the Hokey Pokey as a group and have the child/children take turns holding the shaker container during the dance.
- **Asking Questions to Obtain Information:** Have the child guess what is in the container by listening to the sound it makes and asking questions, such as "Is it something I can eat?" You may want to model the activity first by telling the child what is in the container and asking the child questions to guess the contents.

## COGNITIVE SKILLS:

- **Visual Closure:** Make shapes out of the filler contents, leaving out part of the shape. Have the child finish making the shape.
- **Counting:** Count the filler items as they are placed in the container. Put different amounts in and talk about how it sounds different with concepts such as "many" vs. "few."

## SENSORY:

- **Tactile Exploration:** Allow the child to pick up, run fingers through, etc. different filler items.
- **Auditory Discrimination:** Shake the contents of the container and then present the child again with another container. The child then identifies which one he/she heard the first time. Increase the difficulty by shaking more than two containers.

## ACTIVITY 4

# Hokey Pokey Shapes

## MATERIALS NEEDED:

- Shapes from the templates on pages 56-57 or any other shape items you may have
- Construction paper
- Scissors

## DIRECTIONS:

- Cut out shapes using different colors and sizes
- Sing the Hokey Pokey song using shapes instead of body parts (for example, "Put your circle in, put your circle out, etc.")
- Do the Hokey Pokey with body parts but place the body parts on the shapes (for example, "Put your left arm on the circle, put your left arm on the square, etc."). Place large shapes on the floor to complete the Hokey Pokey this way.

## GROSS MOTOR:

- Sing the song using appropriate body movements for the individual child's skill level and goals.
- Place the shapes in different locations so that the child has to move or reach to touch or retrieve them.

## FINE MOTOR:

- **Tracing:** Allow the child to trace the shapes to make their own shapes for the song.
- **Scissor Skills:** Allow the child to cut shapes as appropriate for his or her skill level.
- Have the child grasp/hold the shape during the song.

## ORAL LANGUAGE:

- **Vocal/Prosody:** Talk about how when we sing the song, we move our body to the beat of the song, and follow the directions.

- **Vocabulary:** Label all the shapes being used and as appropriate, provide labels for more difficult shapes (octagon, hexagon, etc.)
- **Comparison/Same/Different:** Talk about body parts and what shape they are (for example, eyes are round or oval, legs are rectangular, etc.)
- **Phonemic Awareness:** Make up silly phrases using shapes (for example, "Silly squares stand still," "tricky triangles try to tap," etc.)

## WRITTEN LANGUAGE:

- **Pre-Literacy:** Write the names of the shapes on the shapes.

## SOCIAL/PRAGMATIC:

- Talk about how shapes and objects come in different shapes and sizes, just like people.
- **Group Activities:** Talk about how fun the Hokey Pokey is when a lot of people do it together. What are some other games and activities that are more fun with more people?

## COGNITIVE:

- **Generalization/Shape Discrimination:** Give each child a shape and have him/her find an object that is the same shape.
- **Counting:** Have the child count the number of sides of each shape.

## SENSORY:

- **Tactile Exploration:** Give the child objects of different shapes and have her/him describe what they look and feel like.
- **Tactile Discrimination:** Put objects in a bag or box and have the child feel the objects. Can he/she identify the object by shape?

# Shapes

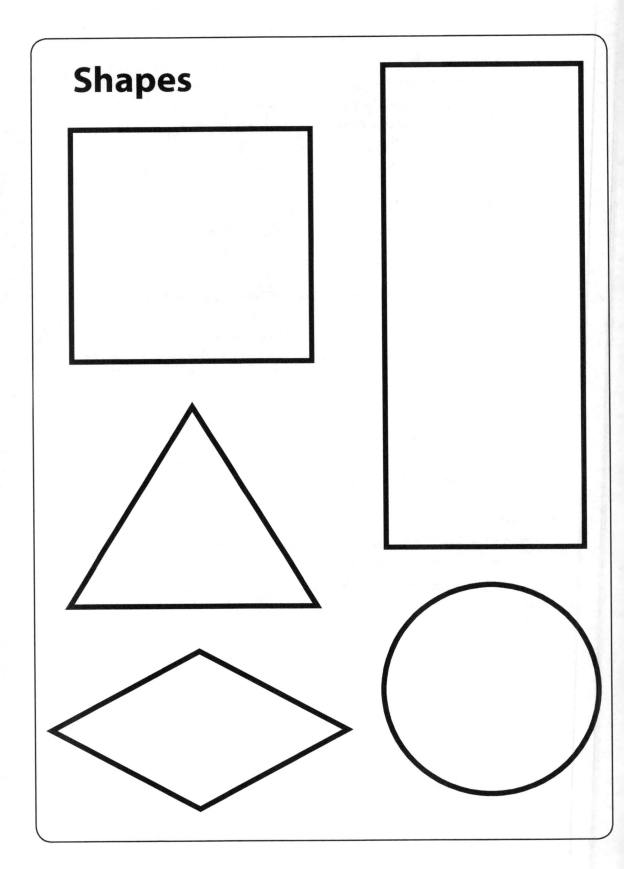

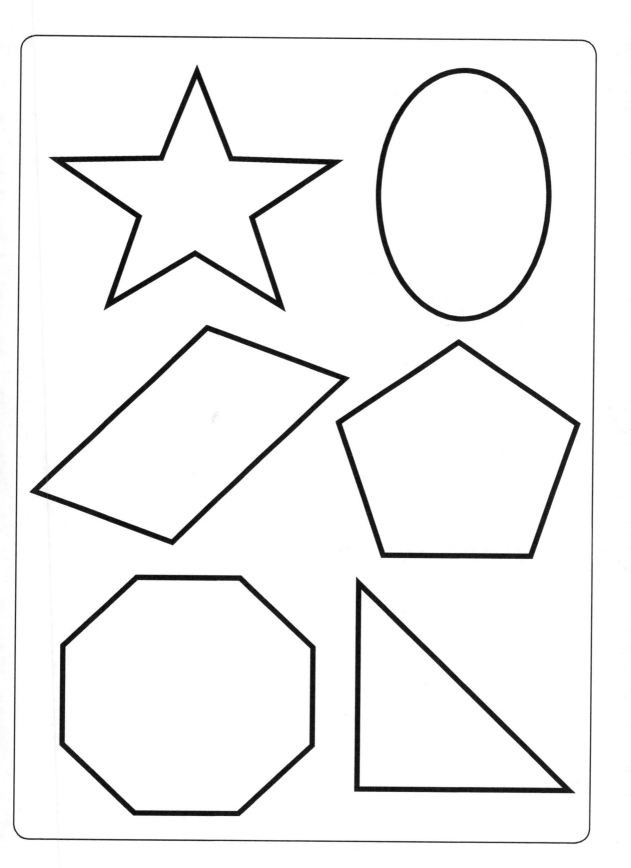

# ACTIVITY 5 — Shake and Make

## MATERIALS NEEDED:

- Printed/copied recipe from page 60
- Small food containers with lids
- One larger food container with lid
- Scoops or measuring cups
- Three to four of the following items:

| | |
|---|---|
| Pretzel sticks | Small snack crackers |
| M&M's® | Raisins |
| Animal crackers | Other snack foods |
| Cereal (Kix®, Alpha-Bits®, Apple Jacks®) | |

## DIRECTIONS:

- Place each of the ingredients into separate small food containers.
- Have the child systematically combine the ingredients into the large container.
- Have the child shake the ingredients together to mix them.
- Have the child use a clean cup to scoop out a serving for him or herself.

## GROSS MOTOR:

- **Balance:** Have the child stand on a rocker board/wobble board or sit on a t-stool/therapy ball as he or she makes the "Shake and Make". The child can shake the ingredients by rolling, jumping, skipping, hopping, etc.

## FINE MOTOR:

- **Pincher Grasp:** Have the child pick out ingredients one at a time and make a face out of the ingredients. Use two M&M's to make eyes, raisins to make a smile, etc. The child can use a scoop, spoon, and other containers to change containers of the "Shake and Make."

# ORAL LANGUAGE:

- **Vocabulary:** Have the child name all the items as he or she adds them to the mixture. Have the child name other items that would be good to add.

- **Action Words:** Have the child describe other ways to mix ingredients (for example, stirring with a spoon, electric mixer, using hands, blender, etc.)

- **Following Directions:** Provide the child with step-by-step verbal instructions while making the "Shake & Make." Directions can be very general or very specific, such as "Add the M&M's" or "Add the green M&M's."

- **Phonemic Awareness:** Have the child rhyme words used within the activity (for example, "spoon, loon, dune, moon" or "shake, bake, lake, take").

# WRITTEN LANGUAGE:

- Write the instructions on the recipe. Have the child cross off each step as he/she completes it.

- Make letters out of the ingredients.

- Discuss the boxes and bags that the ingredients came in. Identify letters on the packages. Talk about how the pictures help identify what is in the package. Ask the child to see if the package has a recipe on it, etc.

# SOCIAL/PRAGMATIC:

- **Manners:** Have the child ask for "some," "more," etc.

- **Team Work:** Pass the container of "Shake & Make" around and have one child hold the container while another child scoops out his/her portion.

- **Turn Taking:** Have each child put in a different ingredient and shake the ingredients together.

# COGNITIVE:

- **Patterning:** Help the child make a pattern using the ingredients. Begin with a simple "AB" pattern. Once the "AB" pattern is mastered, move onto to "ABB" or "ABC" patterns.

- **Sequencing:** Talk about the order the items were put in. Concepts such as first, second, last, etc. can be used.

- **Measuring:** Have the child measure using numbers on the side of a measuring cup. Talk about different measurement amounts, such as a spoon, cup, handful, etc.

# SENSORY:

- **Taste Exploration:** Have the child taste each ingredient separately. Talk about if it's sweet, salty, crunchy, soft, sour, etc.

# Shake and Make

**Ingredients:**

_____   _____
_____   _____
_____   _____
_____   _____
_____   _____
_____   _____

**Directions:**

_____
_____
_____
_____
_____
_____
_____
_____
_____
_____
_____
_____
_____
_____
_____
_____

# ACTIVITY 6

# A Hunting We Will Go
## (Birth - Three Years of Age)

## MATERIALS NEEDED:

- Stuffed animals
- Dolls
- Animal puppets
- Box, laundry basket or pillowcase to put items in

## DIRECTIONS:

- Place different stuffed animals in the box.
- Allow the child to pull out one at a time.

## GROSS MOTOR:

- **Locomotion:** Hide the stuffed animals and dolls around the room. Have the child crawl, roll, or walk to find them.
    - Have the child mimic the movements of the different animals. For example, tell the child to slither on the floor like a snake, waddle like a duck, or crawl on all fours like a bear, dog, or cat.
    - Suggest to the child that he/she can hold the animal and pretend to dance.
- **Body Awareness:** Sing 'The Hokey Pokey' and move the child's body part that corresponds with the song.
    - Sing 'The Hokey Pokey' in front of a mirror so the child can watch him or herself. Point out the body parts referenced in the song in the mirror reflection.
    - Play 'Ring Around the Rosie' using the stuffed animals in the circle.

## FINE MOTOR:

- **Eye/Hand Coordination:** Have the child practice throwing the stuffed animals into the box. Instruct him/her to start with the larger animals and then throw the smaller animals.
- **Pincer Grasp:** Have the child pretend to feed the stuffed animals or toy baby. The child could use a spoon or pincer grasp to feed them.

- Suggest to the child that he/she can dress the animals and dolls. Address skills such as zipping, pulling, buttoning, dressing/undressing, etc.
- Roll out Play-Doh and cut out shapes of animals with the cookie cutters.

## ORAL LANGUAGE:

- **Expressive Language:** Instruct the child to imitate animal noises, such as growling like a bear, barking like a dog, or quacking like a duck.
- Play "peekaboo" with the animals. Hide them under blankets and have the child pull off the blankets and say, "Peekaboo!"
- **Vocabulary:** Have the child name the animals and describe what they look like. Instruct the child to identify body parts on him or herself and on the animals.
- **Phonemic Awareness/Expressive Language:** Sing other songs with animals in them such as, Old MacDonald Had a Farm, The Itsy Bitsy Spider, Five Little Ducks, Mary Had a Little Lamb, The Ants Go Marching, Five Little Monkeys, etc.

## WRITTEN LANGUAGE:

- Have the child name each animal and give it a nametag with its name. Give the child and yourself a nametag as well.

## PRAGMATICS/SOCIAL:

- **Hygiene:** Practice washing different body parts and talking about staying clean.
- **Turn-Taking and Getting Along:** Put the animals in laundry baskets and tie the baskets together with ribbon or string. Have each child pull the "train" with the animals around the room. Talk about sharing the animals and the animals all getting along as they ride in the train.
- **Friendship:** Give "bear hugs" to the animals. Talk about when it is appropriate to hug and touch others.

## COGNITIVE:

- **Matching:** Have the child match the stuffed animal to a picture of a real animal.
- **Following Directions:** Play 'Simon Says' so the child can do tasks with different body parts, for example, "Simon Says blink your eyes; Simon says stomp your feet; Simon Says touch your nose."
- **Concepts:** Put some of the stuffed animals under, on, beside, in front of, and on top of a laundry basket.

# Sensory:

- **Tactile:** Use different objects to rub on body parts when doing the Hokey Pokey, for example, use a feather on the child's foot when he/she puts his or her right or left foot out; a cold washrag on the child's face when he/she puts his or her head in, or place a textured ball in the child's hand when he/she puts his or her right or left hand in.

  - Have the child blow a bubble and then while singing the Hokey Pokey have them pop it with the body part they put in the middle (hand, foot, whole self, etc.)

  - Read Dr. Seuss books such as *The Foot Book* which will reinforce the concept of body parts as well as expose the child to several rhyming words. Another good Dr. Seuss book is *Wet Foot, Dry Foot, Low Foot, High Foot: Learn About Opposites*.

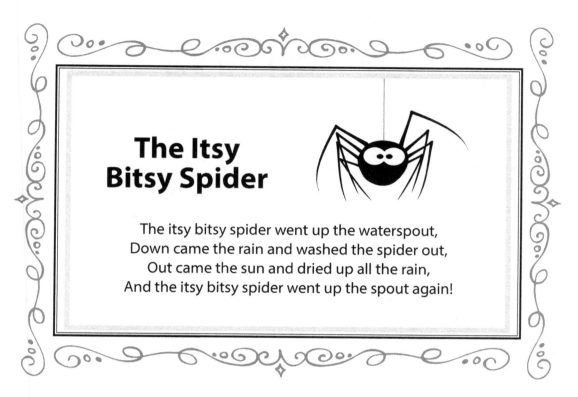

# The Itsy Bitsy Spider

The itsy bitsy spider went up the waterspout,
Down came the rain and washed the spider out,
Out came the sun and dried up all the rain,
And the itsy bitsy spider went up the spout again!

## Directions:

1. Sing the song aloud with the child/children.
2. Hold up a poster with the words of the song on it. Have the children point to each word as you sing the song again.
3. Sing the song again, and have the children participate by voicing and motioning along with you as much as possible. Introduce the finger play to engage the children.

## Suggestions for Hand Motions/Finger Plays:

- Have the children put their thumb and index fingers together to make a "spider." The children can make the spider walk up by rotating their hands to bring their thumbs and index fingers that are on the bottom to the top.
- When the song says, "Down came the rain," have the children make "rain" by putting their hands high up in the air, wiggling their fingers, and bringing their hands down.
- To "wash the spider out," have the children cross their hands in front of them and then move each arm out to the side.
- When the song says "out came the sun," have the children hold their hands over their heads in a circle to make a "sun."
- At the end of the song, have the children make the spider motion again as he crawls back up the spout.

# Make a Pet
# Spider

## MATERIALS NEEDED:

- Spider and water spout template (page 68)
- Glue/tape
- Decorative items:
    - Pipe cleaners
    - Yarn
    - Construction paper
    - Bendable straws
    - Cotton balls
- Scissors
- Markers or crayons

## DIRECTIONS/OPTIONS:

- Copy or print the spider template for children to color/decorate.
- Have the children decorate the spider using either the template spider legs OR by making their own spider legs using the pipe cleaners, yarn, strips of construction paper, or bendable straws.
- The children can then decorate the spider's body by coloring it OR tearing apart a cotton ball and gluing it on the body.

## GROSS MOTOR:

- **Locomotion:** Copy several of the water spout templates from page 68. Place the spouts around the room. Instruct the children to move from spout to spout to move the spider up and down the spout.
- **Core/Proximal Shoulder Strengthening:** The children will be activating/ working their core muscles/shoulders while moving the spider up the spout.

## FINE MOTOR:

- **Scissor Skills:** Have the child cut out the spider or cut the long strips of construction paper to make legs for the spider.
- **Pincer Grasp:** Have the child pull apart the cotton balls then glue the pieces on the spider body.

- Have the child manipulate the legs onto the spider body by bending the straws or pipe cleaners to look like legs.

## Oral Language:

- **Expressive Language:** Talk about where the spider is going as the child moves it up and down the spout. Discuss concepts such as up/down, dry/wet, in/out.
- **Vocabulary:** Talk about vocabulary words such as water spout, itsy bitsy, spider, and other words the child may not know.
- **Rhythm, Prosody, and Voice:** Change the speed of the song from fast to slow; change the volume by singing it soft in certain parts and louder in others.
- **Phonological Awareness:** Have the child make the spider climb other items such as the chair, door, wall, stairs, etc. As the spider is climbing, have the child make rhyming words of what the spider is climbing up: For example, chair/bear, fair/wear, care/dare, door/four, bore/store, more/pour, etc.

## Written Language:

- **Pre-Literacy:** Have the child make letters out of the pipe cleaners.

## Social/Pragmatic:

- **Turn-Taking:** Each child takes a turn making his or her spider climb the water spout as the class sings the rhyme.
- **Asking Questions to Obtain Information:** Hide the spider and model yes/no questions. Encourage the child to imitate or spontaneously ask questions to find it (e.g., "Is it down on the floor? Is it on the water spout? Is it under the table?").

## Cognitive Skills:

- **Counting:** Talk about how many legs the spider has and count them. Look at pictures of other animals and count their legs.
- **Visual Closure:** Make a spider that has the incorrect number of legs. Have the children discuss what is wrong with the spider, and how it should be fixed.

## Sensory:

- **Tactile Description:** Using your hand as a spider, make it crawl up the child's back, leg, arm, etc. and have the child describe what it feels like. You can also use other items to brush on the child, such as a pipe cleaner and cotton ball.

# Spider and Water Spout

## ACTIVITY 2 — Bug Dig

### MATERIALS NEEDED:

- Fake bugs
- Sand, dirt, water, marbles, rice, cotton balls, packing peanuts, etc.
- Medium to large container
- Spoon, tongs, plastic toy spade

### DIRECTIONS:

- Place one of the filler materials in the container.
- Bury the bugs in the filler material.
- Have the child find the bugs by using his/her hands, tongs, a spoon, or a spade.

### GROSS MOTOR:

- **Balance:** Place the container on a counter or table. Have the child stand on a rocker board/wobble board or sit on a t-stool/therapy ball as he or she finds the bugs.
- **Locomotion:** Take the child outside to find either the fake bugs in the container OR place the bugs in the dirt and other places such as on a rock, in a bush, in the sandbox, on the swing, etc.

### FINE MOTOR:

- **Pincer Grasp:** Have the child pick out the bugs with her/his fingers, a spoon, tongs, or a spade. Switch the utensils often to increase skill level.
  - Have the child dig with his/her hands in the filler to find the bugs. Talk about other animals that dig, such as dogs, cats, squirrels, etc.

### ORAL LANGUAGE:

- **Expressive Language:** Talk about where bugs live, what their homes might look like, how many bugs live together, how bugs make their homes, would you like to live where a bug lives, etc.
- **Vocabulary:** Talk about all the different types of bugs (e.g. spider, ant, grasshopper, ladybug, caterpillar, centipede, praying mantis, cricket, lightning bug, etc.). Find pictures of each one and talk about what they look like and where they can be found.

- **Phonological Awareness:** Have the child pick a bug (e.g., a lady bug) and ask him or her to think of other animals that start with the same letter (e.g., lion, lama, loon, lamb, lizard, leopard, etc.)

## Written Language:

- **Writing:** Have the child/children write letters or their names in the dirt during the dig. If you take the children outside, you can also have them practice writing letters in the sand or dirt with a stick/shovel.

- **Letter Matching/Awareness:** Using letters written on paper or alphabet flashcards, have the child categorize the bugs by the first letter of the bug's name by placing the bug next to, under, or on top of the correct letter.

## Social/Pragmatic:

- **Relating to Experiences:** Have the children share or talk about a time that a bug was in their house and what they or their parents did when they found the bug.

- **Teamwork:** Talk about how bugs work together to accomplish tasks such as building homes, finding food, staying safe, etc. Have the children work together to find as many bugs as they can outside, working as a team.

## Cognitive Skills:

- **Generalization:** Have the children compare their own homes to a bug's home. They can talk about what is the same (they sleep there, they live with their family, they collect things there, etc.) and what is different (people eat at a table, bugs hunt for their food, people sleep in beds, bugs sleep on the ground, etc.)

- **Patterning:** Have the child/children line up the bugs they found in the dig from biggest to smallest, and then pattern them making a pattern (ex., ladybug, spider, ladybug, spider, ladybug, spider, etc.)

- **Counting:** Have the children count the bugs as they find them. If you take the children outside, you can also have them count real bugs they find.

## Sensory:

- **Tactile Exploration:** Have the children run their hands through the different filler materials and discuss what each material feels like. Have them talk specifically about water and how that could cause the spider to fall down the spout (because it's slippery and wet, etc.)
  - You can also have the children talk about what they think different bugs would feel like after looking at the pictures. For example, a spider might feel furry, a ladybug would have a hard shell, a caterpillar would be fuzzy, etc.

# Spider Web Weaving

**ACTIVITY 3**

## MATERIALS NEEDED:

- Paper plates
- Licorice (black would be fun!), yarn, string, pipe cleaners, construction paper
- Scissors
- Glue
- Plastic bugs

## DIRECTIONS:

- Have the children cut string licorice, yarn, pipe cleaners, or construction paper to stretch from the middle of the paper plate to outside of the paper plate. Cut enough to cover the paper plate as much as the child would like.
- Glue the pieces from the middle of the plate outwards to make a web-like design.
- Let the children place bugs on the web.

## GROSS MOTOR:

- **Locomotion:** Create a large web on the floor using black string. Have the child maneuver over and around the web using different types of locomotion, such as:

  | | |
  |---|---|
  | Walking | Hopping |
  | Walking backward | Jumping |
  | Walking sideways | Tip-toeing |
  | Crawling | |

## FINE MOTOR:

- **Visual-Motor/Pre-Handwriting Skills:** Have the child color in the middle of the paper plate to create the "body" of the spider. Instruct him/her to use vertical, horizontal, or circular strokes/scribbles to color. Choose a direction that will present an appropriate challenge.

- **Scissor Skills:** Hold the string, licorice, etc. for the child, allowing them to cut the legs for the spider as long or short as they wish. Show them how to cut several legs at one time, for example doubling the string before they cut it.

## ORAL LANGUAGE:

- **Expressive Language:** Describe how the webs look (the shapes of the webs and the shapes within the webs (triangles and circles). Show pictures of real webs and have the children describe those as well, comparing and contrasting with the ones they made. Talk about color, size, shape, etc.
- **Phonological Awareness:** Have the child rhyme words with key words in the song (e.g., spider, spout, sun, itsy, rain). Each time they make a rhyme, they can put on another part of the web or add another bug.

## WRITTEN LANGUAGE:

- On the back side of the paper plate webs, write a large letter. Arrange the plates to make simple words from the songs (e.g., sun, rain, itsy, bitsy, up, down, web). Tell the children to try and find the words on the poster.

## SOCIAL/PRAGMATIC:

- **Generalization/Relating Experiences:** Prompt the children to discuss what a real spider web looks like and why they think spiders make webs (to catch food, for a safe place to live/sleep, etc.). Talk about how we obtain our food, where we live, the differences between safe and unsafe places, etc.

## COGNITIVE:

- **Counting:** Tell the children to count their pieces of licorice or string before putting them on the paper plate. They can also count bugs as they add them to the web, OR you can have the child count the number of times certain words are said during the song (e.g. spider, spout, rain, etc.)
- **Number Recognition:** Write numbers 1-10 the on outer edge of the paper plate and have the child follow the numbers in order as they make the web.

## SENSORY:

- **Tactile Exploration:** Talk about how a spider web feels (sticky) and provide another material to represent the spider web – Silly String® works great!!!

ACTIVITY
4

# Connect
# the Spider

## MATERIALS NEEDED:

- Connect-the-dot spider template on page 76
- Crayons, markers, paint
- Glue stick
- Items to decorate:
    Glitter
    Paper confetti (spider shapes from Halloween would be fun!)
    Coffee beans
    Colored sand
    Yarn

## DIRECTIONS:

- Copy the connect-the-dot spider from the template.
- Have the child connect the dots to make a picture of a spider.
- Have the child color and decorate the spider.
- You can either hang the spider from the ceiling or place it somewhere in the room where a spider might be found.

## GROSS MOTOR:

- **Locomotion:** Place the items needed for completion of the activity in various locations throughout the room. Have the child ambulate (walk, hop, skip, jump, crawl, etc.) to obtain the materials she/he needs.

- **Stair Climbing:** Locate a wall with stairs leading up and down from it, or create stairs using a bench or short sturdy stools. Tape the connect-the-dot spider to the wall. Work on climbing up and down the stairs, placing one foot on each step. Have the child draw the spider, then have him/her color the spider, slowly moving the spider up and down as appropriate.

# FINE MOTOR:

- **Visual-Motor/Pre-Handwriting Skills:** Have the child color the picture using vertical, horizontal, or circular strokes/scribbles. Choose a direction that will present an appropriate challenge.
- **Pincer Grasp:** Have the child use a pincer grasp to pick up small items and to attach them to the spider. Or have the child use tweezers to pick up items.
- **Scissor Skills:** Have the child snip small pieces of colored paper to use as decoration.

# ORAL LANGUAGE:

- **Expressive Language/Speech:** Sing Itsy Bitsy Spider as you and the child complete the activity. Leave out key words and allow time for the child to say or sing them.
- **Description:** Describe how the spider looks as the dots are connected. Have the child talk about what the lines are forming, how the long and short lines look, how the round part is the body, etc.
- Have the child describe what was used to decorate his or her spider. The child can also describe what others used to decorate their spiders.
- **Answering Questions:** Ask the child a question such as, "What is your spider made of? Where does your spider live? Does your spider have two legs?," etc. Allow the child the ask questions as well.
- **Phonemic Awareness:** Make up a silly song about spiders and related items using alliteration. For example, "My silly spider sped slowly" or "The wacky web where Will was."

# WRITTEN LANGUAGE:

- Have the child name the spider he/she made. Write the name of the spider on the paper. Then have the child write his/her own name and compare the letters that make up the names.

# SOCIAL/PRAGMATIC:

- Talk about how when the dots aren't connected, they don't make a picture, however, when they are connected and working together, they make a picture. Talk about how when we work together, we can do things we might not be able to do alone.
- Talk about how if the dots aren't connected in the correct order, the picture may not be correct. Talk about the importance of following directions step by step.

## COGNITIVE:

- **Problem-Solving/Visual Closure:** Have the child guess what the picture is before beginning the activity. As you begin to connect the dots, encourage the child to continue guessing until she/he guesses correctly. Talk about the shape of the picture as it begins to form when connecting the dots.

- **Counting:** Count along with the child as she/he connects the dots. If the child cannot count, provide a visual number line so the child can use it to connect the dots in order.

## SENSORY:

- **Tactile Exploration:** Allow the child to manipulate the decorative items when completing the picture.

- **Auditory:** Talk about how spiders make no sounds. Ask: "What other animals don't make sounds?" and "What animals are very loud?" Have the child identify sounds in the environment that are soft and loud.

# Connect-the-Dot

ACTIVITY 5

# Spider Sundaes/ Parfaits

## MATERIALS NEEDED:

- Clear plastic cups
- Spoons
- Toppings:
  Raisins
  Chocolate chips
  Fruit snacks in bug shapes
  Gummy worms
  Granola, etc.
- Small containers for toppings
- Yogurt/vanilla pudding

## DIRECTIONS/OPTIONS:

- Have the children make parfaits in clear cups. Be sure to tell them to layer or "bury" the toppings, just like bugs beneath the dirt. When they have 2-3 layers of yogurt/pudding and toppings, have them look at what the snack looks like through the outside of their cup.

## GROSS MOTOR:

- **Locomotion:** Place the different materials needed around the room, on tables, on the floor, on furniture, etc. Have the child/children retrieve the items using different forms of locomotion (e.g. walking, skipping, hopping, rolling, walking backwards, crawling, etc.)

## FINE MOTOR:

- **Pincer Grasp:** Have the child use a pincer grasp to pick up toppings and place them in the filling.
- **Forearm Rotation:** Instruct the child to use a spoon or scoop to scoop the ingredients out of small containers and sprinkle them on top of the filling.
- **Self-Feeding:** Have the child/children use a spoon to feed themselves the bug parfait.

77

## ORAL LANGUAGE:

- **Vocabulary/Basic Concepts:** Focus on the basic concepts of the position of toppings (e.g., top/middle/bottom, first/second/third, few/many).

- **Auditory Comprehension:** Provide the directions verbally, starting with one simple step; increase the complexity of the steps as appropriate for the child's abilities.

- **Expressive Language:** Have each child describe how he/she made his or her bug sundae and the ingredients he/she used. Have each child then compare his/her sundae to how others made theirs.

## WRITTEN LANGUAGE:

- **Pre-Literacy Skills:** Use the recipe template to either write the directions or use pictures of the items placed in the correct order. Have the child cross off the item or step after it is completed.

## SOCIAL/PRAGMATIC:

- **Turn-Taking:** If each child is making his or her own sundae, let him/her complete one step, then wait for the other children to each take a turn. Talk to them about sharing and using the time they are waiting for their turn to think about what they want to put in next.

- **Generalizing/Relating to Experiences:** Have each child talk about a time that they helped bake/prepare food at home with their mom or dad. Ask what they did at home that was different and what was the same (did they use any of the same ingredients, did they use the oven or stove at home, did they measure out ingredients, did they use a spoon, etc.)

## COGNITIVE:

- **Counting:** Have the child count toppings (chocolate chips, raisins, fruit snacks, etc.) as he/she drops them onto the sundae.

- **Patterning:** Help the child make a pattern as he/she makes a sundae. For example, have the child put a thin layer of pudding into his/her plastic cup, then chocolate chips, then more pudding, then granola, more pudding, chocolate chips, pudding, granola, etc.

- **Visual Closure:** Position the materials and ingredients so that they are partially obstructed from view as the child looks for them.

## SENSORY:

- **Tactile Exploration:** Allow the child to handle the ingredients with his/her fingers. Talk about how each ingredient feels.

- **Oral Exploration:** While the child eats his/her sundae, talk about the different ingredients he/she tastes and how they feel in his/her mouth.

# Spider Sundaes

**Ingredients:**

_____    _____
_____    _____
_____    _____
_____    _____
_____    _____
_____

**Directions:**

_____
_____
_____
_____
_____
_____
_____
_____
_____
_____
_____
_____
_____
_____
_____
_____
_____

# Shadow Spiders
## (Birth - Three Years of Age)

**ACTIVITY 6**

## MATERIALS NEEDED:

- Flashlight
- Blank wall

## DIRECTIONS:

- Turn off lights in the room.
- Use the flashlight to make shadow spiders using fingers and hands.

## GROSS MOTOR:

- **Locomotion:** Let the child hold the flashlight. Using different forms of locomotion, the child can "tag" different items in the room.
  - Hold the flashlight for the child and allow the child to dance, hop, rock, etc. to make funny shadows on the wall.

## FINE MOTOR:

- **Finger/Hand Coordination:** Show the child how to use his/her fingers and hand to make the spider on the wall. Show the child other shadow animals that can be made.
  - Allow the child to hold the flashlight. Have him/her use two hands or one hand. Talk about holding the flashlight steady, making sweeping movements, moving in a circle, etc.

## ORAL LANGUAGE:

- **Expressive Language:** Make noises for the shadow animals. Even if the animal doesn't make a noise (such as a spider), have the children pretend what a spider might sound like.
- **Vocabulary/Concepts:** Talk about concepts such as light/dark, up/down, side to side, big/little, night/day, etc.

- **Phonemic Awareness/Expressive Language:** Sing other songs and rhymes with rain and water in them (e.g., Rain, Rain Go Away, It's Raining, It's Pouring, Row, Row, Row Your Boat, etc.)

# WRITTEN LANGUAGE:

- **Pre-Literacy:** Pretend to write letters or shapes on the wall using the flashlight.

# PRAGMATICS/SOCIAL:

- **Turn-Taking:** Take turns holding the flashlight for others.
- **Team Work:** Using the flashlights, allow several students to make shadows on the wall. Talk about how the children can make the shadows interact and move together on the wall.

# COGNITIVE:

- **Following Directions:** Instruct the children to make or move certain body parts while they are making the shadows.

# SENSORY:

- **Tactile:** Create different light levels in the room (dark, no lights but with the blinds open and the sun coming in, all the lights on, etc.). Talk about what happens to the shadows when different types of light are present.

# If You're Happy and You Know It

If you're happy and you know it,
**CLAP YOUR HANDS**, (clap hands twice)
If you're happy and you know it,
**CLAP YOUR HANDS**, (clap hands twice)
If you're happy and you know it,
Then your face will surely show it, (point to face)
If you're happy and you know it,
**CLAP YOUR HANDS**. (clap hands twice)

**Other verses:**
If you're happy and you know it,
**STOMP YOUR FEET**, (stomp feet twice)
If you're happy and you know it
**SHOUT "HURRAY**!" (shout "hurray!")
If you're happy and you know it,
**DO ALL THREE**.
(clap hands twice, stomp feet twice, shout, "Hurray!")

1. Sing the song aloud with the child/children.

2. Using the poster, have the child/children point to each word as you sing the song again.

3. Teach the children the ASL sign for 'happy' and then use it as they sing the song. The sign for "happy" is made by placing one or both of your hands in front of you, palms facing you. Move your hands in a circular motion forward, down, back, up, forward, down, back, up. Both hands move at the same time and in the same direction. On the upward swing, the hands are very close to your chest or touch your chest. On the downward swing, your hands are further away from your chest.

## Suggestions for Hand Motions/Finger Plays:

- Have the children complete the directions in the song (clapping hands, pointing to their faces, stomping their feet, etc.)

# Put Your Best Face Forward

**ACTIVITY 1**

## MATERIALS NEEDED:

- Face template from page 86
- Popsicle sticks
- Glue
- Scissors
- Crayons, markers
- Yarn (for hair)

## DIRECTIONS:

- Copy the face template, one for each child.
- Cut the face templates out, or have the children cut out the faces.
- Have the children decorate their faces with a smile, eyes, and nose. Encourage them to make the faces look like their own. They can then add the yarn to make hair.
- Have the children glue the popsicle sticks on the faces so they can hold them.

## GROSS MOTOR:

- **Locomotion:** Place the faces across the room and instruct the children to walk, run, skip, hop, etc. over to the faces to pick out the one that is their face, or their friend's face, etc. You can also give more specific directions, such as "If you're happy and you know it, find a redhead," or "If you're happy and you know it, find blue eyes." Then the children can race to the correct faces.
- You can change the directions in the song to have the children do large motor movements. For example, "If you're happy and you know it, jump up high, bounce on a ball, crawl on the floor, skip around the room, roll on the floor, etc."

## FINE MOTOR:

- Have the child use fine motor skills to glue, draw, cut out the project, etc.
- Instead of gluing the items/decorations on the faces, use Velcro. Then, give the child directions on what objects to add and remove from their face. For example, "If you're happy and you know it, put on brown hair."

## ORAL LANGUAGE:

- Talk about the different emotions people can have, such as happy, sad, angry, etc. Then have them use the emotion words in sentences, such as, "When I'm sad, I cry." You can even have them act out the words, for instance, they could use a happy voice to say "I'm happy," or a sad voice to say, "I'm sad."

- Talk with them about how they know how others are feeling. Have them explain how they know when their mom is mad, or when their sister is being silly, etc.

- **Vocabulary:** Introduce different emotion words. You can have the children group the words into categories, such as words that mean the same as sad, etc.

## WRITTEN LANGUAGE:

- **Alphabet Identification:** Using alphabet cut-outs or flash cards, play a game with the children in which you say, "If you're happy and you know it, find the 'H'," Go through the different letters of the alphabet.

- **Pre-Literacy:** Going through a book, have the children identify pictures of people who are happy, sad, angry, etc. Have them practice how to hold a book correctly, how to read from left to right, etc.

## SOCIAL PRAGMATIC:

- Using a mirror, talk about how your face can show how you feel. Have the children look in the mirror and make faces that show they are happy, sad, angry, scared, etc. They can also hold up the face they made in the mirror and compare it to their own face.

- Have the children make another face on the back of their project so that they have one happy face and one sad face on their templates. Then ask them questions such as, "How do you feel when your mom makes your favorite meal to eat?" and have the children show the appropriate side of their face template.

## COGNITIVE SKILLS:

- Mix up a face (ex. having the parts in the wrong places), and then have the child fix it to make it correct.

- **Visual Closure:** Present half of a finished face (e.g. the left side), then instruct the child to finish making/drawing the rest of the face.

## SENSORY:

- Have the children touch something of a specific texture while singing the song. For example, "If you're happy and you know it, touch something soft/touch something cold/touch something hard, etc."

# Face

**ACTIVITY 2**

# Put on Your Happy Face

## MATERIALS:

- Brown paper bags (either lunch size, grocery size, or both)
- Crayons, markers, etc.
- Decorative items, such as yarn, bows, buttons, etc.

## DIRECTIONS:

- Instruct the children to draw/decorate faces on the paper bags to show different emotions.

## GROSS MOTOR:

- Have the children walk around the room and find objects that make them feel like the emotion on their bag. When they find an object, have them put the item in their bag.
- Have the children display different movements that correlate with the different emotions. For example, they can stomp to display anger, jump up and down to display feeling happy or lay down/crawl to show sadness.
- Play music or sing, and have the children dance their paper bag puppets around the room.

## FINE MOTOR:

- Have the children use fine motor skills to decorate their bags using markers, glue, etc.
- To make the puppets talk, the children will use their hands inside the bag to control the puppet's mouth.
- Have the children make a puppet show and explain how to make the puppets look like they are actually talking (moving the puppets' mouths to correlate with their speech, bouncing the puppet up and down).

## ORAL LANGUAGE:

- Children can use the puppets to have a conversation with each other.

- Have the children practice using different voices. For example, the children can make the puppets talk loud or soft or sound angry, be silly, etc.

- Have the children make the puppet talk about how they feel today and why. You can also carry over the conversation to include different situations, such as how you feel on a rainy day, etc.

## WRITTEN LANGUAGE:

- Write the emotion that is being portrayed on the bottom of the bag. Have the children copy the letters in the word.

- Have the children practice writing their own names on the back of the bag so they know it's theirs.

- Have the children practice finding letters in words on the bag that are in their name. For example, a child named Hank could look for the 'H' in happy.

- **Sentence Completion:** Have the children fill in the end of a sentence with an emotion word. For example, "Sarah is _____." Have cards of words that are emotions, including happy, sad, silly, etc.

## SOCIAL/PRAGMATIC:

- Have the child ask others (classmates, mom, dad, siblings, etc.) what things make them happy or sad and compare those things to their own thoughts and emotions.

- Have the children make a puppet show and talk about how to be a good friend. Ask them to portray how they can tell how their friends are feeling based on what they say or how they act.

- Have one child act out an emotion, then have the other children find the face displaying that emotion.

## COGNITIVE:

- Have the children categorize their bags into similar emotions and discuss how the words mean the same thing.

- **Size Discrimination:** Have the children identify the differences between the large and small sacks/puppets.

## Phonological Awareness:

- **Rhyming:** Sing the song with a difference (e.g., "If you're happy and you know it, say a word that rhymes with big."). Have the children shout out the rhyming words.

## Sensory:

- Talk about how different sensory stimulations can make you feel. For example, you can ask the children how they feel when they are cold, how they feel when they touch something sticky or too hot, are warm under a blanket, etc.

# ACTIVITY 3 — My Happy Book

## MATERIALS NEEDED:

- Template from pages 92-93 or paper folded over to make a book
- Crayons, markers, colored pencils
- Old magazines
- Scissors
- Tape or glue

## DIRECTIONS:

- Either cut out the copies from the template to make enough for a book, or use blank white paper folded over to make a book.
- In the book, the child can designate pages for specific emotions, such as happy, sad, etc. and find things to glue or draw on each page.
- Have the child look through old magazines to tear out or cut out pictures that make them happy.
- The child can also draw pictures of what makes them happy/sad, etc. throughout the book.

## GROSS MOTOR:

- **Core/Proximal Shoulder Strengthening:** The child will be activating/working his or her core muscles and shoulders while drawing against the wall.
- **Balancing:** Have the child sit on a large ball rather than a chair to work on balancing while they make their book.

## FINE MOTOR:

- Tearing, cutting, spreading out glue and taping are all fine motor coordination activities.
- Have the children draw pictures in the book of what makes them happy to work on their drawing skills.

## ORAL LANGUAGE:

- Have the child explain why they put each picture where they did.

- Have the child dictate a story using the pictures in the book to make up a story line. You may write the sentences that correlate to the story so that they can share it with others.

- **Same/Different:** Have the child share their book with others. Have them tell what makes their friends happy. They can talk about things that are the same in their book as others, and what things are different.

- When looking through the magazines, have the child look at pictures and describe how the person in the picture is feeling, and how they know that.

## WRITTEN LANGUAGE:

- **Pre-Literacy:** While looking through the magazine, have the children find words such as "happy" or "sad" and cut out those words to put in their book.

- Have the child dictate a sentence for each page in the book. Write the sentence at the bottom of the page for the child.

## SOCIAL/PRAGMATIC:

- **Generalizing Situations:** Have the child talk about a time when they felt a specific emotion, such as anger. Have them tell what happened in that situation and how it felt. You could also have them talk about what they did to change or keep that emotion.

- The therapist or teacher can talk about things that the children do that make them happy or upset.

## PHONEMIC AWARENESS:

- Have the children find words that rhyme with pictures in their book.

## COGNITIVE SKILLS:

- **Patterning:** Have the children put pictures of things in order (for example: happy-happy-sad, happy-happy-sad).

## SENSORY:

- Hide the child's book somewhere in the room. As he or she is searching for the book, clap softy when he or she is far away and clap loudly when they get close to the book. Talk about distinguishing loud and soft sounds. You can also use other techniques, such as fast and slow clapping, or saying the words loudly then softer.

# My
# Happy
# Book

By: _____

# Emotions
# Memory Game

## MATERIALS NEEDED:

- Emotion face cards from template on pages 97-98
- Card stock
- Scissors
- Crayons, markers

## DIRECTIONS:

- Copy the emotion face cards from the template, making sure you have two of each (using cardstock to copy the template face card works best).
- Cut out each card.
- Have the child color the card.
- Using an appropriate number of matching pairs for the child's skill level, turn the cards over so they are face down.
- Play the memory game and try to match the emotion faces.

## GROSS MOTOR:

- Have the child work on the cards and play the game while sitting on a therapy ball or t-stool.
- After the child makes a match, have the child perform the appropriate actions, for example, he or she can jump up and down, give a "high five," or do a dance to show they are happy.

## FINE MOTOR:

- **Scissor Skills:** Allow the child to cut out game pieces as appropriate for his/her skill level.
- **Forearm Rotation:** Tell the child to turn the cards over, providing appropriate assistance as needed.
- **Visual-Motor/Pre-Handwriting Skills:** Have child color the game pieces using vertical, horizontal, or circular strokes and scribbles. Choose a direction that will present an appropriate challenge.

## ORAL LANGUAGE:

- Talk about the different emotions as you cut, color, and play the game. Talk with the children about how we can tell emotions by looking at people's faces and body movements.

- **Same/Different:** Show the child the cards in pairs and talk about how the pairs will be the same. Ask the child how we can tell that things are the same or different. Talk about other items or pairs of items that are the same (e.g., shoes, gloves, socks, skates, earrings, chopsticks, headlights, crutches, etc.)

- When a child finds a match, have him/her name things or describe situations that make him or her feel that emotion. For example, the match for happy could be "birthday party, visit from grandparents, new pet," etc.

- **Phonemic Awareness:** Have the child make rhyming words for the emotions they match. For example, "sad, fad, lad, mad, rad, pad, tad," etc.

## WRITTEN LANGUAGE:

- Write the name of the emotions on the bottom of the card. Encourage the child to use the words to help with matching.

## SOCIAL/PRAGMATIC:

- **Turn Taking:** Talk to the child about how you need to take turns in order to play the game appropriately.

- **Following Rules:** Talk with the child about how important it is to follow the rules of a game. Talk about how it is no fun if you cheat, and that others won't want to play with you if you don't follow the rules of the game, etc.

- **Sportsmanship:** Talk with the child about how you can have fun with the game, whether you win or lose. Talk about how there will be times that everyone wins and loses and that you need to be a good sport either way. For example, talk about not bragging when you win and not getting mad when you lose.

## COGNITIVE:

- **Patterning:** Have the child make a pattern with the cards. For example, "happy/sad/happy/sad."

- **Visual Memory:** Cue the child to utilize memory techniques while playing the game. For example, "I saw the other happy face in the bottom row," or "Do you remember where you saw the sad face?"

# SENSORY:

- **Auditory Discrimination:** Talk about how certain sounds are associated with different emotions. For example, when you laugh you are happy, when you are sad you cry, when you are surprised you gasp, etc. Make the sounds and have the child determine what emotion you are expressing. You can also have the child make the sound and you guess the emotion.

## ACTIVITY 5 — What a Sweet Smile

**MATERIALS NEEDED:**

- Sugar cookie
- Icing
- Decorations: Raisins, sprinkles, candy pieces (Red Hots®, hard candy, etc.), nuts, cereal, and anything else you can use to decorate the cookies.
- Plastic knife

**DIRECTIONS:**

- Spread some icing on a sugar cookie.
- Allow the child to decorate a face on the cookie.

**GROSS MOTOR:**

- Have the child decorate a cookie while sitting/balancing on a ball, standing/stretching at a counter, or while sitting cross-legged on the floor, etc.
- Have the child retrieve each item for decorating in different areas of the room, at different heights, etc. The child can skip, hop, roll, walk backwards, etc. to locate and bring back each item.

**FINE MOTOR:**

- Allow the child to spread icing over a cookie with the plastic knife.
- Have the child sprinkle and/or place items on the cookie to form a face by using his or her thumb and fingers.
- Allow the child to open the icing container by pulling off its lid and the sprinkles container by twisting it off.

**ORAL LANGUAGE:**

- Have the child ask for each ingredient that he or she wants to use. You may need to model the correct verbal response for the child.
- Have the child describe what he or she is doing with each step of the decorating. You can also "think aloud" as you decorate your cookie (e.g., "I'm using the knife

to spread the pink icing"; "I'm sprinkling the red sprinkles all over the cookie"; "I'm making a happy face with the Red Hots", etc.)

- **Following Directions:** Describe to the child step by step what you want him or her to do to the cookie (e.g., use the knife to spread the icing, scrape the icing off the knife, open the bottle of Red Hots, make eyes with the Red Hots, etc.)

## WRITTEN LANGUAGE:

- **Pre-Literacy Skills:** Write down the items that will be used to decorate the cookie on a list. As each item is used, have the child cross it off the list, or have the child cross off the labels on the containers as they use each item.

- Allow the child to ice the cookie and write a letter in the icing using his finger. He could write the first letter of his name, the first letter of the alphabet, etc.

- **Phonemic Awareness:** Each time the child uses an item (i.e., icing, sprinkles, candy, etc.) have him or her make up several words that rhymes with each one.

## SOCIAL/PRAGMATIC:

- **Sharing:** Have the child decorate a cookie for a friend, a parent, teacher, etc. Tell the child to give the cookie to the recipient and explain what it is, how he or she decorated it, why he or she decorated it for that person, etc.

## COGNITIVE:

- **Problem-Solving:** Set-up situations where the child is unable to complete a task (e.g., spreading icing with a plastic knife or popsicle stick). Have the child problem solve what else he or she could do or use to spread the icing on the cookie.

- **Counting:** Have the child count how many children use each item to decorate their cookie (e.g., how many children used red sprinkles, how many used M&M's, Red Hots, etc.)

## SENSORY:

- Tell the child to feel the different textures of the decorations on the cookies. Talk about how the different things feel, taste, smell, look, etc.

- Have the children shake the different containers of the ingredients and talk about the sounds they make (e.g., sprinkles, Red Hots, etc.)

# What a Sweet Smile

**Ingredients:**

_____        _____
_____        _____
_____        _____
_____        _____
_____        _____
_____        _____

**Directions:**

_____
_____
_____
_____
_____
_____
_____
_____
_____
_____
_____
_____
_____
_____
_____
_____
_____
_____
_____

## ACTIVITY 6

# The Happy Dance
## (Birth to Three Years of Age)

## MATERIALS NEEDED:

- Music (you can choose different rhythms and tempos)
- Footprint template on page 104
- Scissors
- Markers

## DIRECTIONS:

- Play the music while you sing the song. Make sure the rate/rhythm of the song matches the music as you sing it.
- You may have the children dance around to the tempo of the music.
- Cut out the footprint template to be used during the activities. You can also trace the children's actual feet and cut those out to use.
- If you are working with an infant, you can move his or her arms and legs to the music, rock, or dance while you are holding him or her.

## GROSS MOTOR:

- **Locomotion:** The children will be dancing. You can teach them different dance steps, such as the Macarena, The Chicken Dance, The Cha-Cha, the Slide, etc.
- You can also tell the children to follow the footprints on the floor to make a dance.
- With infants, you can sing the song with different variations and move the child when directions in the song are given. For example, "If you're happy and you know it, roll on your side."

## FINE MOTOR:

- Help the children to clap their hands together. You can also incorporate other directions into the song. For example, you tell the child to wiggle his or her fingers, wipe the table, etc.
- If you have the children trace their own feet, you can have them help you hold the pencil and trace, or trace each other's feet.

## ORAL LANGUAGE:

- Have the children make an animal sound as the song is sung. For example, "If you're happy and you know it, be a cow—Moo!"

- Start out singing and leave off the last word for the child to fill in. Have the child decide what action should be inserted to the song.

- Have the children ask each other to dance or to join a group. You may have to model how to appropriately ask these questions.

## PHONEMIC AWARENESS:

- Have the children count out the beat of the song by clapping their hands on their legs as they sing. For younger children, you can swing them or rock them to the beat of the song.

## WRITTEN LANGUAGE:

- Using a picture book, have the children look at pictures of people who are happy. You can also point to pictures.

- Draw or paste pictures of different instruments on the footprints. When the children hear that particular instrument used in the music, they can step on the footprint that corresponds to it.

## SOCIAL/PRAGMATICS:

- Have the children dance with partners. Teach them that it is appropriate to ask: "May I cut in . . ." in order to dance with someone who already has a partner, and, "Would you like to dance?" to ask someone to join you dancing.

- For younger children, work on eye contact and facial expressions while dancing with them.

## COGNITIVE:

- **Following Directions/Counting:** Place footsteps on the floor with numbers on them for the children to place their feet on in the correct order to make a dance.

- **Patterning:** Have the children clap/stomp out a pattern while the music is playing (e.g., clap, clap, stomp).

## SENSORY:

- Talk about the rate and volume of the music. Talk about how you use your ears to hear. While listening, the children can try to pick out what instruments they hear.

# Footprints

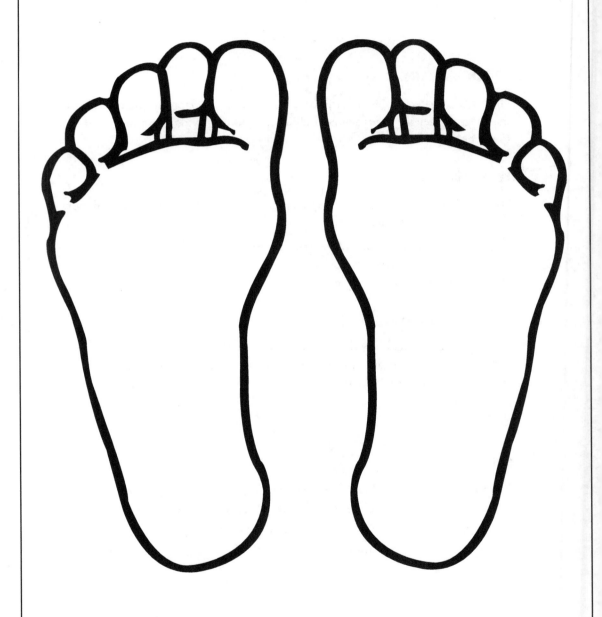

# The Alphabet Song

A – B – C – D – E – F – G – H – I – J – K – L – M – N – O
P – Q – R – S – T – U – V – W – X – Y and Z.
Now I know my ABCs,
Next time won't you sing with me?

1. Sing the song aloud with the children.

2. Using the poster, have the children touch each letter with their fingers while singing the song.

3. You can hang the poster on something magnetic, such as a chalkboard, and then have the children use letter magnets to put on the poster or take down as each letter is said.

4. Put the poster on the floor (or make your own letters on the floor with masking tape) and have the children take turns jumping onto each letter as it is sung.

## Suggestions for Hand Motions/Fingerplays:

- Have the children sign the alphabet in ASL as they say each letter. See page 106 for the letter signs.

- Have each child raise their hand when the letter that starts the beginning of their name is sung.

# Sign Language Alphabet

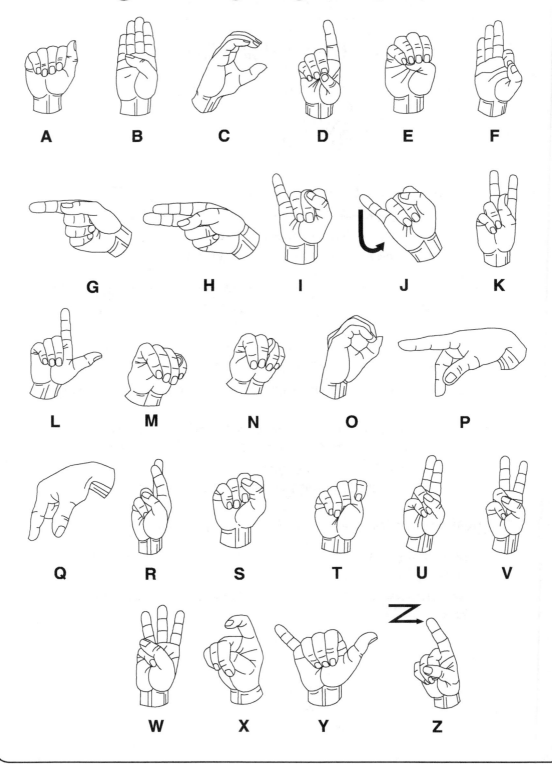

# ACTIVITY 1

# My Letter Book

## MATERIALS NEEDED:

- Book template from pages 109-110 or white paper to make your own book
- Alphabet letters template from pages 111-112
- Markers, crayons, colored pencils
- String, pipe cleaners, yarn, ribbon, etc. to tie the book together
- Paper punch to make holes

## DIRECTIONS:

- Have the children fold their book and then help them tie it together.
- For the inside of the book, children can cut, color, and paste letters from template on page 111-112 OR
  - Practice writing their own letters throughout the book.
  - Find pictures in magazines to cut out that start with certain letters.

## GROSS MOTOR:

- Have the children sit on a balance ball while making their books.
- Have the children focus on finding verbs or actions that start with certain letters while looking through magazines (e.g., "jumping" for "j" and "walking" for "w"). If they can't find pictures, they can make their own drawings. Then, while reading the book, they have to complete all of the actions as they go.

## FINE MOTOR:

- Have the children put their books all together, practicing their cutting, coloring, tearing out pictures, writing, etc.
- After showing the children how to tie the ribbon, yarn, etc. for their books, you can have them work on tying their shoes, or tying a ribbon in a doll's hair, etc.

## ORAL LANGUAGE:

- For each page in their books, have the children formulate a sentence using a word that starts with the corresponding letter. Write the sentence on the page for them.

- **Vocabulary:** Instruct the children to think of as many words as they can that start with each letter in their book.

- Talk about the alphabet with the children. Discuss how the letters go in a certain order, how there are big and little letters, and other things that go in a certain order, such as numbers, the days of the week, months of the year, etc. You can also talk about other concepts, such as how names go in alphabetical order when attendance is called.

- Have each child hide a letter behind his or her back. Tell the other children to ask questions to determine what letter the child is (e.g., "Are you a consonant or vowel? Do you have a circle in your letter?"), etc.

## PHONEMIC AWARENESS:

- Have the child clap as he/she says each letter.

## WRITTEN LANGUAGE:

- Have the children practice writing their own letters to match the letters in the book. Tell them to decorate or trace their letters.

- **Pre-Literacy:** Have the children flip through a magazine searching for letters. Have them cut out all the different variations, fonts, and sizes of letters and talk about the different ways letters can be made.

## SOCIAL/PRAGMATIC:

- Talk about how letters make words, and using words is how we get things done. Stress how everyone needs to work together to get things done and we communicate by using our words.

- Tell the children how each letter is important, just like every person.

## COGNITIVE:

- **Visual Memory:** Place 3-4 letters on the floor. Tell the children to close their eyes. Remove one of the letters, then ask the children which letter you removed.

- **Patterning:** Use letters to make patterns, either using different letters or upper and lower case letters.

## SENSORY

- Use different textured letters or materials to make the letters and glue them on the pages (e.g., cloth letters, fur, foam letters, sandpaper, glue sand, or sprinkles in the shape of letters). Then have the children talk about the different textures and the colors of the letters.

# My
# Letter
# Book

**By:** _____

# Alphabet

A B C D
E F G H
I J K L
M N O

# PQRS
# TUVW
# XYZ

ACTIVITY
2

# Alphabet
# March

## GROSS MOTOR:

- Have the children march, skip, hop, etc. around the room while singing the ABC's. Work on marching to a beat, raising one leg for each letter, etc.

- **Locomotion:** Have the children walk up a flight of stairs and stick a letter from pages 111-112 on the wall as they climb each stair, OR have the children say a new letter for each stair they climb.

- Put magnetic letters up high on a chalkboard/refrigerator and have the child reach to get them down.

## FINE MOTOR:

- Have the children pick up letters out of a bucket and put them on a magnetic board.

- Instruct the children to use tweezers or tongs to pick up the letters and put them on or take them off the board.

- Place wooden beads with letters on them around the room. Have the children march around to get them and then string them together.

## ORAL LANGUAGE:

- **Following Directions:** Tell the children what letter to look for or to find an object that starts with a certain letter, and have them follow your directions.

- **Vocabulary Development:** Have the children march around the room and find something that they don't know the name of. You tell the child what it is, what letters are in its name, and what you do with it. Then, you look for an unnamed object that the child describes to you.

- **Concept Development:** Have a discussion with the children about things that stick and how they think magnets might work. Talk about what magnets stick to and what they don't stick to, etc.

## PHONEMIC AWARENESS:

- On the march, have children find objects that start with a certain sound and bring them back to you.

## WRITTEN LANGUAGE:

- Give the children a card with a certain letter on it. Make the sound the letter makes, and then have them find an object in the room that starts with that letter. Have the children put the letter on the object.

- Place the lowercase letters around the room. Give the children the uppercase letters and have them find the lowercase letters that match.

## SOCIAL/PRAGMATICS:

- Talk to the children about putting things away and why there is a place for everything. Have the children be sure to put back any items they use in the activities in their correct places.

- **Problem-Solving:** While taking a walk, talk about things that you see that aren't safe. Talk about how you can tell someone when you see something that's not safe and what you should do in those situations.

## COGNITIVE:

- **Visual Memory:** After the children have marched around the room and looked at things, have them close their eyes. Remove something from the room. Tell them you removed something that starts with the letter 'B' and tell them to find what you removed.

- Talk about what letters the names of colors start with. Name a letter and have the children say what colors start with that letter. Then tell them to find an object that is that color.

- **Visual Closure:** Instruct the children to put together a wooden puzzle of letters to make a whole picture.

## SENSORY:

- **Tactile:** While the children are on their hunt, have them find something that is hard, soft, smooth, cold, etc.

- Tell the children to close their eyes and give them an object. Have them feel it and describe it to guess what it is and what letter it starts with. Then, close your eyes and have them give you an object to guess.

# ACTIVITY 3

# "I Spy" Label Looking

## MATERIALS NEEDED:

- Paper towel or toilet paper roll
- Tape/construction paper to make a telescope
- Objects in the environment

## DIRECTIONS:

- Tell the children to look through their telescopes to find things in the environment that start with certain letters or find letters throughout the room (on a calendar, chalkboard, etc.)

## GROSS MOTOR:

- **Locomotion:** Have the children march, hop, or skip around with their telescopes to get to different areas of the room to look for things.
- Tell the children to squat low to look for things, or stand up on their tippy-toes to look for objects.
- Outside, have the children use sidewalk chalk to make large alphabet letters on the ground as they "spy" them with their telescopes.

## FINE MOTOR:

- Have the children make their own telescopes using paper and then gluing or taping it.
- The children can decorate the telescope by coloring the paper before they roll it up.

## ORAL LANGUAGE:

- Whenever the children spy something, they have to describe what they are seeing to have someone else guess what they are looking at.
- After the activity, have the children sit in a circle and discuss what they spied. Start with "a" and have the children work all of the way through the alphabet. Have the children say, "I spied something that started with the letter 'B' and it was a boat."

- Have the children tell a story that includes as many words as they can that start with the same letter. For example, they can talk about a dog named Dan who went to a dance. The story could be told round-robin style or each child could tell a story using a different letter.

## WRITTEN LANGUAGE:

- Have the children write all the letters of the alphabet on their telescope.

## PHONOLOGICAL AWARENESS:

- Have the children say, "I spy something that starts with the sound ___" and have the other children try to guess what it is.
- Have the children make up a silly rhyme in which all or most of the words start with the same sound/letter, for example, "Paul picked pretty pansies for poor Polly."

## SOCIAL/PRAGMATIC:

- Talk about why it's not nice to spy on people or watch them when they don't know it. Talk about how it makes you feel when someone is doing that to you.

## COGNITIVE:

- **Colors:** Have the children "I spy" things that are certain colors.
- **Counting:** Have the children count the number of things around the room using their telescopes, for example, suggest that they count how many chairs are in the room, etc.
- **Concentration:** Make a memory game with the letters from template 111-112. Cut out two of each letter and have the child play memory.

## SENSORY:

- Talk about the concepts of light and dark. Create different lighting environments in the room and talk about how that affects what you can see (e.g., have all of the lights on, open the window, but turn the lights off, have one light on, etc.)
- Using Play-Doh, shaving cream, sand, squeezable jelly, or ketchup, have the children write letters. Talk about how the different textures feel, etc.

## ACTIVITY 4 — Letter Toss

### MATERIALS NEEDED:

- The alphabet poster
- Things to toss
  Beanbags
  Small stuffed animal
  M&M's®
  A sock (rolled into ball)

### DIRECTIONS/OPTIONS:

- Place the poster on the floor or on a table.
- Allow the child to toss the beanbag or other object onto the poster.
- When the beanbag lands on a letter, name the letter for the child, name the sound the letter makes, and have the child come up with words that start with that letter.

### GROSS MOTOR:

- Have the child(ren) sit or stand as appropriate for his/her developmental skills while tossing the bean bag. You could have the child stand backwards and throw it over his/her head, to the side, under his/her leg, etc.
- Have the child move to different locations to toss the beanbag. Have her/him use different modes of locomotion to get to the different areas.
- Have the child stand on a t-stool or a therapy ball to throw the bean bag.
- Have the child move farther away from the poster. Talk about how you will have to throw the beanbag harder or softer in order for it to land on the poster appropriately.

### FINE MOTOR:

- Have the children throw or toss the beanbag using different hand grasps. For example, they could hold it in the palm of their hand, using the pincer grasp, or by using either her/his dominant or non-dominant hand.
- Have the children trace the letter that the bean bag lands on with their hand or finger.

- If you use rolled-up socks for the activity, allow the children to form the sock into a ball shape.

- Have the children retrieve the beanbags or objects after they have been thrown. They can use their hands, feet, or other things (tongs, tweezers, clothespins, etc.) in order to pick up the object. They could even use a broom to "sweep" the objects off of the poster!!

## ORAL LANGUAGE:

- Encourage the children to come up with multiple words for each sound/letter. Provide new vocabulary words that start with those sounds for the children.

- **Vocabulary:** Talk about the action words/verbs used during the activity with the children, such as toss, throw, pitch, etc.

- When the children land on a letter, teach them the ASL sign for that letter. Encourage the children to use the signs for letters they know while singing the alphabet song.

- **Phonemic Awareness:** Have the children make a silly sentence for whatever sound they land on. For example, "Abby ate an apple."

- **Categories:** When the children land on a letter, give them a category that the word they say must come from. For example, "Name an animal that starts with 'B', or "Name a fruit that starts with 'S'." You can also use other categories, such as colors, candy, girls'/boys' names, body parts, etc.

## WRITTEN LANGUAGE:

- When the beanbag lands on a letter, have the children find another word that starts with the same letter. You could find this word on labels, magazines, signs, in books, bulletin boards, etc.

## SOCIAL/PRAGMATIC:

- **Strategies/Problem-Solving:** Have the children share strategies that worked for them while throwing the bean bags. Talk about what you could do if the beanbags go too far (i.e., don't throw it as hard) or if they don't go far enough (throw it harder), etc.

- Talk about when it is ok to throw things and when it's not. Explain to the child that you can usually throw things outside, but not inside, how you shouldn't throw things at people, and how there are some things you can't throw because they would break, etc.

## COGNITIVE:

- **Concepts:** Talk about the concepts of beside, next to, and beginning, middle, and end. When the children toss the bean bag, talk about what letter is beside the one it landed on, what letters come before and after it, what letters are at the beginning and end of the alphabet, etc.
- **Counting:** Have the children count the letters of the alphabet.

## SENSORY:

- Have the children close their eyes or blindfold them when throwing the bean bag. Talk about how hard it is to throw the beanbag without being able to see.

## ACTIVITY 5 — Alphabet Sticks

### MATERIALS NEEDED:

- Pretzel rods
- Peanut butter, frosting
- Alpha-Bits® Cereal (or Fruit Loops®, sprinkles, crushed cookies, mini-chocolate chips, etc.)
- Plastic knife
- Wax paper
- Recipe template on page 123, write ingredients and directions

### DIRECTIONS:

- Tear a large piece of wax paper off and place it on a flat surface.
- Spread the Alpha-Bits® cereal (or other items) on the wax paper.
- Spread the peanut butter or frosting on the pretzel rod.
- Roll the pretzel over the cereal so that the cereal sticks to the pretzel.

### GROSS MOTOR:

- **Locomotion:** Have the children find the ingredients needed for this activity. Place the items up high (on the counter), down low (under counter in cabinet), in various spots around the room.
- **Balance:** Use masking tape to make a long line on the floor. Provide the children with a spoon and Alpha-Bits cereal. Show them how to walk the line holding the spoon with the cereal in it.

### FINE MOTOR:

- Allow the children to spread or apply the peanut butter or frosting with various techniques (for example, they could use a plastic knife to spread, use their fingers to spread, dip a pretzel in a container with the peanut butter/frosting, roll the pretzel to cover it, have one child hold the pretzel while another child spreads, etc.)
- After the peanut butter/frosting is on the pretzel, have the child roll the pretzel in the cereal, sprinkles, crushed cookies, etc.
- Allow the child to pick the cereal off the pretzel and eat it.

## ORAL LANGUAGE:

- **Concepts:** Talk about concepts such as in/out of the jar, on/off the pretzel, verbs such as rolling, sticking, picking, spreading, eating, etc.

- Talk about where peanut butter comes from. How/where peanuts are grown, the differences between crunchy & smooth, how it's made, different name brands, etc.

- Have the child describe what they are doing with each step of the activity. For example, "I'm using the knife to spread the peanut butter on the pretzel,"; "I'm rolling the pretzel in the cereal to cover it," etc. You may need to model these utterances or expand on utterances the child says. For example, if the child says, "I rolling pretzel," you can say, "Yes, you are rolling the pretzel in the cereal."

- Have the children describe the boxes/packaging the ingredients come in. Talk about different aspects of the packaging, such as the colors used, the pictures, games on the boxes, etc.

## PHONEMIC AWARENESS:

- **Segmenting:** Have the children clap the syllables in words such as pretzel, peanut, butter, frosting, spread, cereal, knife, rolling, etc.

- **Rhyming:** Have the children make up rhymes that correspond with the action words used in the activity. For example, words like "roll, spread, bite, eat, stick, etc."

## WRITTEN LANGUAGE:

- Have the children try and spell out their names using the Alpha-Bit cereal. Or if you use Fruit Loops, have the children make letters using the cereal.

- Using the recipe, have the children cross off each step as it is completed.

- Have the children identify letters on labels for the foods used in the activity, such as peanut butter, cereal boxes, frosting can, etc. You can also talk about what numbers mean in terms of nutrition, what ingredients are, and where to find them on the jar, etc.

## COGNITIVE:

- **Generalization:** Have the children talk about other things they might use with peanut butter or frosting. For example, peanut butter and jelly sandwiches, 'ants on a log', icing a cake, icing cookies, etc.

- **Sorting:** Have the children sort the cereal. It can be sorted by color, size, letter, type, etc.

## SOCIAL/PRAGMATIC:

- Talk with the children about meal times and snack times. Talk about how we communicate with each other during these times, how food is used during many social activities, and why.

- **Problem-Solving:** Discuss the importance of following a recipe. Talk about why we use a recipe to make foods, what happens when you don't follow the recipe, what you can do when you don't have an ingredient, etc.

## SENSORY:

- Have the children talk about or eat the cereal when it's dry. Then, put the cereal in milk and let it get soft. Talk about the difference between crunchy and soft and why/how that happens. Have the children talk about other words you could use to describe the different textures.

- Put out different types of pretzels (e.g. twists, sticks, rods, braids). Talk about the differences when they bite into the different kinds and about how the different kinds look, feel, etc.

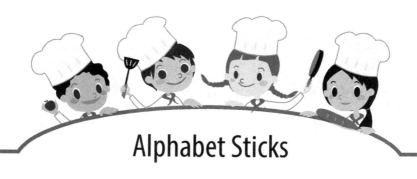

# Alphabet Sticks

**Ingredients:**

_____        _____
_____        _____
_____        _____
_____        _____
_____        _____
_____

**Directions:**

_____
_____
_____
_____
_____
_____
_____
_____
_____
_____
_____
_____
_____
_____
_____
_____
_____

# ACTIVITY 6

# A-B-C Sock!!
## (Birth-Three Years of Age)

## MATERIALS NEEDED:

- At least one sock, any size will work
- Permanent markers, fabric paint

## DIRECTIONS:

- Use the markers (all different colors look great!) or the fabric paint to write the alphabet letters all over the sock.
- After the letters dry, put the sock on your hand (if the child is very young) or on the hand of the child (if he is older).
- Use the sock as a puppet and have it sing the Alphabet song with you and the child.

## GROSS MOTOR:

- **Locomotion:** Place the alphabet puppet in different locations and have the child find it as you both sing the song. When he/she finds it, then the puppet can sing along!
- Have the child walk, hop, jump, skip, etc. with just socks on, socks and shoes, and bare feet. This is great for sensory too!

## FINE MOTOR:

- **Daily Living/Dressing:** Have the child take off and put on socks, including the alphabet sock. He/she can also practice other dressing activities as appropriate for each child's goals.
  - Have the child put the sock on his hand and move it to make the puppet sing or talk. If the child is not old enough to do this on his own, you make the puppet talk or sing using your hand. Put the puppet close enough to the child so that he/she can try and grasp it, move it to initiate head or eye movement from the child, etc.
  - If the child is old enough, allow him/her to try and write the letters on his/her puppet.

## ORAL LANGUAGE:

- **Vocal/Prosody:** As you sing the song, move the puppet in a rhythmic motion, encouraging the child to sing along with you. Make the puppet become very excited, moving and jumping around when the child makes noise or sings along.

- Use the puppet to talk with the child. It can ask questions, teach new words, ask him/her to sing along with it, etc. If the child is old enough, he/she can make his/her own puppet talk. Have a puppet show!

- With young children, show them where their socks go. Show them their feet, your feet, etc. Maybe do "This Little Piggy" or have the puppet do it! Let them try and pull off their socks. It's a great time to talk about other articles of clothing such as pants, shirts, shoes, etc.

- **Phonemic Awareness:** For younger children, hold their hands and clap along with the song as you sing. Older children can clap for themselves, even having their puppet help!

## WRITTEN LANGUAGE:

- **Pre-Literacy:** Use the board books with letters (dollar stores are great places to find these!) and point to the letters as you sing. Or the puppet can take the child's hand and follow along with the letters.

## SOCIAL/PRAGMATIC:

- **Eye Contact:** Sing the song to and with the child. Make sure to make eye contact and encourage eye contact from the child. Use the puppet to redirect the child's head if eye contact is lost.

- **Turn-Taking:** Sing the song to the younger child, stopping every 3 or 4 letters, and let the child respond either verbally or with a gesture, facial expression, etc. Provide immediate verbal feedback and reinforcement, and then continue the song.

## COGNITIVE:

- Sing the song to or with the child. When you sing, "Won't you sing along with me," substitute the child's name.

- **Counting:** Sing the song using numbers instead of letters.

## SENSORY:

- Sing the song at different speeds and volumes, moving the child's body or the puppet along with the rhythm. Talk with the child about the differences in the songs.

- As you and the puppet sing the song, use the puppet to brush against different body parts for sensory stimulation.

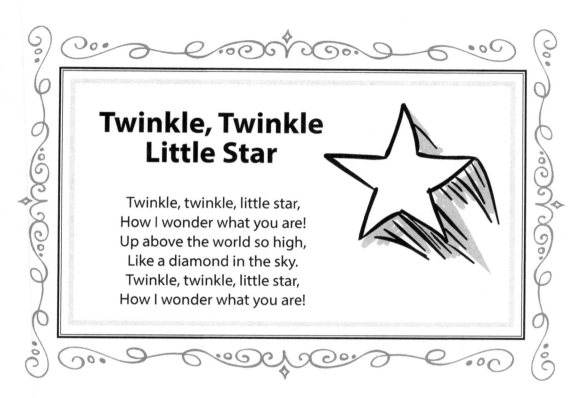

# Twinkle, Twinkle Little Star

Twinkle, twinkle, little star,
How I wonder what you are!
Up above the world so high,
Like a diamond in the sky.
Twinkle, twinkle, little star,
How I wonder what you are!

1. Sing the song aloud with the children.

2. Sing the song aloud again. Using the poster, allow a child to help you point to each word as it is said. Let him/her use his/her finger, flashlight, or even better, put a **STAR** on the end of a pointer. A wand from a Halloween costume would be great!!

3. Sing the song again and have the children participate by singing along and moving along with you as much as possible. Introduce hand gestures/finger plays to engage the children.

## Suggestions for Hand Motions/Finger Plays:

- Hold out your hands and make them "twinkle" by wiggling your fingers.
- Sign "star" by pointing both index fingers up, then move one up, then down, then other fingers up and down.
- Hold your hands out to the side, palms up, as if asking a question.
- Put your index fingers together and your thumbs together and push to make a diamond shape.
- Hold your arm way up high, moving it back and forth, with your index finger pointing up.

# 1 Shapes Mobile

## MATERIALS NEEDED:

- Shapes templates (pages 56-57)
- Markers or crayons
- Single hole punch or clear tape
- Decorative items:
    Glitter
    Paint
    Stickers
    Sequins
    Colored sand
    Cereal with shapes (Fruit Loops®, Lucky Charms®, Alpha-Bits®, etc.)
    Tinfoil
- Small pieces of paper or tissue paper

- Scissors
- String or yarn
- Plastic coat hanger or paper plate

## DIRECTIONS/OPTIONS:

- Copy or print the shapes templates. You can have the children decorate the shapes using markers, crayons, or another medium of your choice. Have the children cut out the shapes if age-appropriate.
- Cut the string or yarn of varying lengths.
- Put a hole in each of the shapes using the hole punch and tie the yarn/string through it. If you don't have the hole punch, tape the shapes to the string/yarn with clear tape.
- Tie the other end of the yarn on the coat hanger, or cut holes around the edge of the paper plate and tie the string/yarn through those holes.
- Hang up the mobile/s around the room so that the children can see them!!

## GROSS MOTOR:

- Have the child hang his or her own mobile up by standing on their tiptoes or using a step stool or other appropriate device.
- Hang the mobile up and have the child reach for the shape that you name. If appropriate, the child can jump, run and jump, hop, etc. to reach for the shapes.

# FINE MOTOR:

- **Scissor Skills:** Allow the child to cut out the shapes if appropriate. The child can also snip small pieces of tin foil, tissue paper, colored paper, etc. to use as the decoration.

- **Pincer Grasp:** Have the child use a pincer grasp to pick up small items (sequins, cereal, stickers, etc.) and to attach them to the stars.

- **Tying Skills:** Allow the child to tie the string/yarn to the shapes and to the coat hanger/paper plate.

- Have the child fold the decorative items (see above) before gluing them on shapes. Or have the child fold the shapes and see what other shapes they make after they are folded.

- **Visual-Motor/Pre-Handwriting Skills:** Instruct the child to trace around the inside edge of the shape.

# ORAL LANGUAGE:

- **Expressive Language:** Talk about other things you can see in the sky at night (moon, clouds, etc.). Then talk about things you can see in the sky during the day. Go outside for a walk and name all the things in the sky (cloud, sun, airplane, bird).

- **Phonemic Awareness:** Talk about rhyming words. Point out rhyming words in the song (star/are, high/sky). Have the child come up with his/her own rhyming word (true or nonsense word):

    Star/are
        Which word rhymes with star: far, play, eat
        Say another word that rhymes with star: _____
    High/sky
        Which word rhymes with high: stay, fry, sun
        Say another word that rhymes with high: _____

- "Wh" Questions: Point out the "wh" question (what) in the song and discuss. Talk about the stars, where we find stars, when we see stars.

- Concepts: Substitute other "size" words for "little" while singing the song. Words like big, huge, gigantic, humongous, mega, large (opposites) or tiny, small, teeny, mini, itsy bitsy, etc. Talk about how changing the word changes how the song sounds and changes the meaning of the song.

# WRITTEN LANGUAGE:

- **Pre-Literacy:** Write the name of each shape on the shapes of the mobile. Allow the child to trace the word with crayons or their finger. Talk about the beginning sounds of each, how the words are made up of letters, see if any of the letters match letters in the other shape words, etc.

## SOCIAL/PRAGMATIC:

- **Turn-Taking:** Have each child take a turn hanging his/her mobile. The child can tell which shape he or she likes best on the mobile and why.

- **Sharing:** Have the children use shapes that others have cut and decorated on their mobiles. Trade a diamond for someone else's diamond, a circle for someone else's circle, etc. Talk about how the shapes made and decorated by someone else are different and the same.

## COGNITIVE SKILLS:

- **Problem-Solving:** Talk about how we find things and information when we don't know about something. Help the child brainstorm ways to find information such as asking an adult, using a map, checking on the Internet, searching in books, etc.

- **Patterning:** Help the child make a pattern using the shapes. Begin with an "AB" pattern, asking the child to continue the pattern you begin, or create his/her own pattern. Once the "AB" pattern is mastered, move onto "ABB" or "ABC" patterns.

- **Sorting:** Cut out extra shapes and have the child sort shapes, putting them in piles, or making a mobile with lots of one shape.

- **Following Commands:** Ask the child to follow simple commands such as "Draw a circle on the star" or "Draw a square on the triangle," etc.

## SENSORY:

- **Tactile Exploration:** Use small items of varied textures (e.g., tinfoil, sequins, glitter, cereal) as decoration.

## ACTIVITY 2 — Star Maker

### MATERIALS NEEDED:

- Large piece of blue or black construction paper
- Scissors
- Tape
- Materials to cut out or make stars:
  - Tinfoil
  - Cloth
  - Colored paper
  - Magazines
  - Sponge
  - Markers
  - Paint
  - Pipe cleaners
  - Star stickers

### DIRECTIONS:

- Hang a large piece of black or blue paper on the wall or bulletin board.
- Use the Star Template (page 134) to cut out more star shapes using the materials.
- Have the children tape the stars onto the large piece of construction paper.
- Children can also draw or finger paint the star shapes directly on the large piece of construction paper. Star stickers or pipe cleaners can also be used to make star shapes.

### GROSS MOTOR:

- **Locomotion:** Direct the children to perform a movement or action each time they move to place another star on the paper:

  | | |
  |---|---|
  | Walk forward | Hop on one foot |
  | Walk backwards | Hop on two feet |
  | Run | Gallop |
  | Skip | |

- **Balance:** Have the child stand on a rocker board/wobble board or sit on t-stool/therapy ball as he/she places the stars on the paper.

# FINE MOTOR:

- **Visual-Motor/Pre-Handwriting Skills:** Have child color the stars using vertical, horizontal, or circular strokes/scribbles. Choose a direction that will present an appropriate challenge.
- **Scissor Skills:** Allow the child to cut out the stars.

# ORAL LANGUAGE:

- **"Wh" questions:** After the stars are placed on the large piece of paper, ask the child "wh" questions about the stars. For example, "Where is the blue star?"; "What is the shiny star made of?"; "Why did you put the little star there?," etc.
- **Vocabulary:** Talk about other items we find in the sky (moon, sun, birds, planes, etc.) and add them to the large piece of paper.
- **Concepts:** Talk about concepts such as up/down, big/little, here/there, above/below, far/near. Place stars around the room to demonstrate these concepts (e.g., the child can place one star 'here' and another star 'there'—across the room by a particular item or landmark). Or place the stars on the large piece of paper to demonstrate the concepts, such as "Put the blue star below the red star."
- **Phonemic Awareness:** Have the child clap with each syllable until he/she hears or sings the word 'star', then he/she can tape the stars on the large piece of paper.

# WRITTEN LANGUAGE:

- **Pre-Literacy:** Instruct the child to look through a magazine looking for pictures of stars. When he or she finds a picture of a star, tear or cut it out and put it on the large piece of paper. Talk about literacy skills such as looking at books from front to back, using pictures to comprehend what is happening, turning pages one at a time, identifying individual letters and words, etc.

# SOCIAL/PRAGMATIC:

- **Generalizing:** Tell the children to talk about the times they have seen things in the sky or maybe even been in the sky (on a plane). Have them describe what it felt like or maybe what it would be like to be a pilot or astronaut.
- **Turn-Taking:** Instruct the children to take turns putting their stars on the paper. After each child puts his or her star on the paper, he or she may choose the next child to put his or her star up.

# COGNITIVE:

- **Following Directions:** Provide verbal directions to the child such as, "Put the star on the left side of the paper", "Point to all the little stars", "Show me the stars that are beside each other," etc.

- **Patterning:** Have the child place items in patterns such as star-star-moon, little star-big star-little star, etc.

- **Counting:** Have the child count all the stars or stars in more specific categories such as little stars, stars made of tin foil, stars that are yellow, etc.

- **Visual Memory:** As the child looks at the board with the stars and other items on it, tell him/her to close his/her eyes. Take an item off the board and see if the child can find what was taken off.

# SENSORY:

- **Visual:** Describe a star to the child and see if he/she can point to the one you are describing.

# Stars

## ACTIVITY 3 — Wall of Stars

### MATERIALS NEEDED:

- Star template (page 134)
- Pictures of famous people (even the children in the class!), places, and things – use a magazine.
- Glue or tape
- Scissors
- Clear plastic wrap
- Decorative items:
    Glitter
    Yarn
    Sequins
    Star stickers
    Tinfoil
    Pasta
    Wrapping paper

### DIRECTIONS/OPTIONS:

- Copy or print the star template.
- Tell each child to cut out the star, or cut the star out for the child.
- Find pictures of famous people, places, or things, cut them out, and paste them to the star. You can use pictures of the children too!!
- You can decorate the star before putting on the pictures by using the tin foil, wrapping paper, etc.
- Decorate the star after the picture is glued on. Make it look glamorous with glitter, star stickers, etc.
- Cover the star in clear plastic wrap to make it look like it's covered in glass!!
- Put the "stars" on the wall, refrigerator, bulletin board, etc.

### GROSS MOTOR:

- Have the child put his/her star at different heights on the wall. Each child will need to stand on tiptoe, squat down, or walk side-to-side to place the stars in a line.

- **Locomotion:** Take the stars and place them on the floor. Have the child move from star to star using different types of locomotion. They can hop, walk, run, place stars close together for baby steps, far apart for large steps, etc.

# FINE MOTOR:

- **Pincer Grasp:** Have the child decorate the star with sequins, pasta, etc. using a pincer grasp.
  - Have the child attach a star to a bulletin board using a push pin or to a dry erase board, magnetic board, or attach to refrigerator using a magnet.

# ORAL LANGUAGE:

- Talk about the famous people, things, etc. that the children chose. Ask them what 'famous' means and what makes something or someone famous?
- Talk to the child about what he or she thinks it would be like to be famous. Would he or she like to be famous?
- Talk about the different meaning of the word 'star'. Talk about other words that sound the same but have different meanings, such as 'play', 'store', 'ball', 'bark', 'bob', 'bat', 'bear', 'bridge', 'gum', 'mold', 'page', 'well', etc.
- **Phonemic Awareness:** Use the star's name to generate words that rhyme. For example, ask the child or children, "Find words that rhyme with 'Oprah.'" You can use either the first or both the first and last names. For example, "Find words that rhyme with 'Brad Pitt'" and the child could respond with "Mad Hit." Make up new fun names for the stars!!
- **Phonemic Awareness:** Have the children find a star that has a name that begins with the same letter as their first name.

# WRITTEN LANGUAGE:

- **Pre-Literacy:** Allow the child to flip through the magazine. Talk with him or her about turning pages carefully one at a time, the beginning and end of the magazine, how letters make up the words, using pictures to understand the magazine, etc.
- Instruct the child to write or copy the star's name on the bottom of the star.

# SOCIAL/PRAGMATIC

- Have the child share with others why they chose the person, how they decorated the star, why they chose the colors, etc.
- Talk to the children about people who do great things every day and are not famous (people like firemen, policemen, teachers, doctors, parents, etc.)

- **Generalizing/Relating to Experiences:** Ask the children to share if they have ever met anyone famous, or if they could meet anyone famous, who would it be?

## COGNITIVE

- **Categorizing:** Instruct the children to place the stars in categories such as famous people, famous places, famous animals, famous cartoon characters, etc.

- **Counting:** Have the children count how many are in each category (i.e., how many famous people do we have?, etc.)

- **Visual Closure:** Partially obstruct the picture of the famous star and have the child guess who or what it is.

# ACTIVITY 4 — Constellation Creation

## MATERIALS NEEDED:

- Star template from page 134.
- Construction paper
- Scissors
- Crayons
- Magnets
- Dry erase board, cookie sheet, refrigerator, black board

## DIRECTIONS/OPTIONS:

- Cut the star from the template to make lots of stars out of the construction paper.
- Attach the magnets to the back of the stars.
- Have the children place the stars so that they form different shapes (star, square, heart, triangle), constellations (like the Big Dipper), or simple designs (a flower, face, house, etc.).

## GROSS MOTOR:

- Have the child place those stars in the constellation that challenge his individual gross motor skills. For example, if the child is working on squatting, he/she puts the stars on the lower part of the constellation.
- Tell the child to make a "shooting star" by placing stars way up high and then gradually decreasing the height of the stars until they reach the ground.

## FINE MOTOR:

- Allow the child to place the magnets on the back of the stars.
- Have the child remove the stars one at a time with alternating hands.
- Let the child trace around the stars onto the construction paper to make all the stars for the activity.

## ORAL LANGUAGE:

- **Vocabulary:** Talk about what a "constellation" is. What other words mean the same thing ('group', 'collection', etc.)? Ask what other words deal with space ('satellite', 'space ship', 'galaxy', 'planet', 'shooting star', 'comet', etc.)

- Talk about "wishing on a star." Ask the children to explain what a wish is, what each of them would wish for, and whether wishes really come true, etc.

- Talk about the picture that was created by using the stars. Ask: What is it? What does it do? Where do we find it? etc.

- **Phonemic Awareness:** After each picture is made, clap out the syllables in that word, talk about what sounds we hear in that word, and find other words that start with the same sound.

## WRITTEN LANGUAGE:

- Have the children practice making letters out of the stars.

## SOCIAL/PRAGMATIC:

- Talk about how the individual stars make up a larger picture. Then talk about how each individual makes up larger groups, such as a family or class.

- **Teamwork:** Have the children agree upon a shape or picture to make. Then have the children make the picture as a team, with each child making a star to be used as part of the bigger picture.

## COGNITIVE:

- **Visual Closure:** Start to make a picture using the stars, putting one star up at time. Have the children guess what picture is being made after each new star is added.

- **Counting:** Count the number of stars in each constellation. Talk about how a bigger picture would take more stars, and how a smaller picture would take fewer stars.

## SENSORY:

- **Tactile Exploration:** Have the child feel a shape with his or her eyes closed. See if he or she can describe or tell what shape it is and have him or her recreate it using the stars.

# Snack Fit for a Star

## MATERIALS NEEDED:

- Bread
- Jelly
- Peanut butter
- Cookie cutters (all shapes)
- Plastic knife
- Recipe template on page 142, with written ingredients and directions

## DIRECTIONS:

- Spread the peanut butter on one piece of bread.
- Spread the jelly on the other piece of bread.
- Put them together to make a sandwich.
- Allow the child to cut out shapes from the sandwich using the cookie cutters.

## GROSS MOTOR:

- Allow the children to help find and bring back the ingredients needed for the recipe. Have them use different types of locomotion as they retrieve and bring back the ingredients.
- Allow the children to stand on stools or other steady objects while they are cutting out their shapes.

## FINE MOTOR:

- Tell the children to spread their own peanut butter and jelly if they are able, or use a hand-over-hand technique to help the child spread the ingredients.
- Instruct the children to remove and replace the tie from the bread sack and open the jars of peanut butter and jelly.
- Ask the children to help wash the cookie cutters at the sink.

# ORAL LANGUAGE:

- **Phonemic Awareness:** Sing the song 'Peanut Butter and Jelly' as you make the sandwiches. Talk about how the rhythm of that song is different than the rhythm of 'Twinkle Twinkle Little Star'.

- Talk about the different types of peanut butter and jelly that are being used (e.g., crunchy vs. creamy, types of jelly—strawberry, grape, apple butter, etc.)

- **Concepts:** Talk about the different types of containers that the ingredients came in (bag, plastic jar, glass jar, squeeze bottle, etc.). Talk about why the jar would not work for the bread, why the squeeze bottle won't work for the peanut butter, etc. Have the children describe the differences between the containers.

- **Following Directions:** Verbally provide steps to completing this recipe. Then have the children retell the steps as you make your sandwich.

# WRITTEN LANGUAGE:

- **Pre-Literacy:** Write the items that will be used to complete the recipe on a list. Allow the child to cross off the item after it has been used.

- **Pre-Literacy:** Have the child look at the labels identifying letters or words he or she may recognize, talk about the information that is provided on labels, etc.

# SOCIAL/PRAGMATIC:

- **Sharing:** Talk with the children about how everyone can share the peanut butter, jelly, and bread and still have enough for everyone. Talk about taking "only what you need."

- **Manners:** Talk to and model for the children how to ask for items that they need. For example, "Can you please pass the jelly?"

# COGNITIVE:

- **Problem-Solving:** Ask the children to guess what step or ingredient will come next.

- **Generalizing:** Talk with the children about what other types of sandwiches could be made this way. For example, bologna with cheese.

# SENSORY:

- While eating the snack, talk about the different flavors of the ingredients (e.g., crunchy vs. creamy, different flavors of jelly, how the peanut butter tastes different than the jelly).

- Allow the children to explore the texture of the ingredients by touching them. Make shapes using the jelly on a finger, etc.

# Snack Fit for a Star

**Ingredients:**

_____  _____
_____  _____
_____  _____
_____  _____
_____  _____
_____  _____

**Directions:**

_____
_____
_____
_____
_____
_____
_____
_____
_____
_____
_____
_____
_____
_____
_____
_____
_____

# Star Gazing
## (Birth — Three Years of Age)

## MATERIALS NEEDED:

- Blanket
- Pillows
- Fan
- Flashlight
- Wind chimes

## DIRECTIONS:

- Lay the blanket and pillows on the floor or outside if possible.
- Lay on your back with the children and sing Twinkle, Twinkle, Little Star as you're looking for stars.
- Use the additional materials to simulate being outside. For example, turn the fan on to simulate the wind, move the wind chimes to make a "twinkle" noise, and use the flashlight to simulate the stars or moon.

## GROSS MOTOR:

- Address skills such as rolling, crawling, and rocking on the blanket.

## FINE MOTOR:

- **Pincer Grasp:** Allow the child to hold the flashlight or use a hand-over-hand technique to assist the child.
- Place the wind chimes over the child so he or she will reach for them or try to make them move.
- **Pointing:** Have the children point to the "stars" or "moon" or make their fingers point for them. You can also encourage them to make shapes in front of the flashlight that will be reflected on the ceiling!

## ORAL LANGUAGE:

- **Verbal Expression:** Encourage the child to sing along with you. If he is unable, hum the song to elicit verbalization.

- **Rhythm/Prosody/Phonemic Awareness:** Sing the song, emphasizing the pitch and intonation changes. Move the child's arm or legs in rhythm with the song.

- **Vocabulary:** Repeat key vocabulary words found in the song after singing it. Explain the words while doing the simulations. For example, talk about the wind, how it is blowing, how it feels, etc. while the fan is on.

- Sing the song, leaving off some key words. Encourage the child to complete the phrase of the song. For example, "Twinkle, twinkle, little _____."

## WRITTEN LANGUAGE:

- **Pre-Literacy:** Look at a children's book with stars in the pictures. Let the child turn the pages and encourage them to point to the pictures.

## SOCIAL/PRAGMATIC:

- **Turn-Taking:** During the simulation point out where you see stars, how the "wind" feels and then tell the child to locate stars, tell how the wind feels, etc.

- **Eye Contact:** Encourage the child to look at you if he or she is not looking at the stars.

## COGNITIVE:

- **Attention to Object:** Move the flashlight, chimes, etc. to different positions around the child's body so he or she can locate the object.

- **Visual Scanning:** Move the objects from side to side and in other directions to elicit visual scanning.

## SENSORY:

- Wrap or tuck the blanket around the child during the activity.

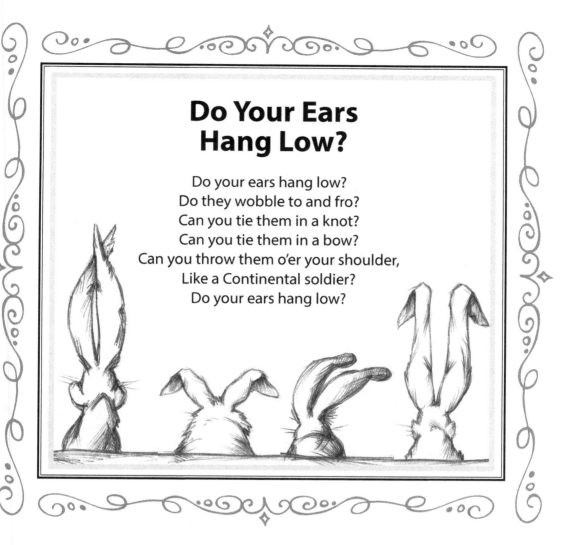

# Do Your Ears Hang Low?

Do your ears hang low?
Do they wobble to and fro?
Can you tie them in a knot?
Can you tie them in a bow?
Can you throw them o'er your shoulder,
Like a Continental soldier?
Do your ears hang low?

1. Sing the song aloud with the child/children.

2. Sing the song again, using the poster, and have the child follow along with the words using his/her finger, a pointer, or flashlight.

3. Sing the song a third time and have the child/children participate by voicing and motioning along with you as much as possible. Introduce hand gestures/finger plays to engage the children.

## Suggestions for Hand Motions/Finger Plays:

- Point to ears when you say "ears".
- Move your hands from side to side when you say "wobble to and fro."
- Make a tying motion and pretend to tie a bow.
- Toss your clasped hands over your shoulder.
- Salute when you sing "continental soldier."

# Like an Animal

## MATERIALS NEEDED:

- Animal ear templates page 150
- Crayons/markers
- Construction paper
- Decorative items:
  Pipe cleaners
  Felt/foam board
  Buttons
  Yarn
  Cotton balls
- Paper plates
- Glue
- Scissors

## DIRECTIONS/OPTIONS:

- Copy the animal ear templates using construction paper.
- Cut the ears out for the children or allow them to cut them out themselves if they are able.
- Glue the ears on the back of the paper plate at the top where the ears should go.
- Allow the children to make the face of the animal by either coloring the eyes, nose, and mouth, or by using decorative items to create the face.

## GROSS MOTOR:

- **Locomotion:** After the children have completed their animals, have them move like different animals (e.g., hop like rabbits, slither like snakes, crawl like turtles, etc.)
- **Stair Climbing:** Locate a wall with stairs leading up and down from it or create stairs using benches or stools. Tape the pieces of the activity on the wall and have the child climb the stairs or bench to take off the pieces (paper plate, ears, etc.). After he/she acquires each piece, he/she can use it to decorate the paper plate.

# Fine Motor:

- **Scissor Skills:** If the child is able to make consecutive snips to cut through paper, have him/her cut out the ears. A hand-over-hand technique can be used with a child unable to cut independently.

- Practice tying shoes while singing the song.

- Allow the children to decorate their paper plates. Have them use a pincer grasp or tweezers to pick up the decorative items.

# Oral Language:

- **Description:** Ask the children to talk about the animals they made: What kind of animal is it? What does it look like? What sounds does it make? How does it move? What does it eat? Where does it live? etc.

- **Concepts:** Talk about long/short ears, floppy/straight ears, small/big ears, etc.

- Talk about what we do with our ears and how animals use their ears.

- **Body Parts:** Sing the song, substituting different body parts.

- **Phonemic Awareness:** To the rhythm of the song, move "to and fro" using the animals the children made.

# Written Language:

- Print the name of the animal each child made on its own index card. Place the cards where the children can see them and have them try and find the word corresponding with animal that they made. Give cues like, "The elephant will be a long word" or "Pig has three letters."

- Write the child's name on the back of the paper plate animal he/she made. See if he/she can recognize it. Allow the child to trace the letters.

# Social/Pragmatic:

- Talk about the different groups that animals live in. For example, fish live in schools, geese live in a gaggle, wolves live in packs, etc. Talk about why animals live in groups. Do humans live in groups? What do we call these groups (families, cities, states, etc.)?

- Talk about how different people have different types of body parts. Talk about how the animals have different types of body parts (e.g., dogs have different types/sizes of ears and tails). Discuss how being different is a good thing and how teasing someone who is different is not appropriate.

## COGNITIVE:

- **Same/Different:** Have the children compare their animals (e.g., how are the animals' ears the same and different (size, shape, etc.). Talk about other animals and look at pictures for ears that are the same or different.

- **Visual Closure:** Use two different animal ears on the paper plate with a face that matches one of the animals. Have the child decide which ear should be used.

- **Categorizing:** Have the child/children put the animals in different categories such as farm animals, zoo animals, pets, etc.

## SENSORY:

- **Auditory:** Make or tape-record different animal noises. Have the child identify which animal it was.

- **Sensory:** Encourage the children to use different textured materials to create their animals.

# ACTIVITY 2
# All About Ears Hunt

## MATERIALS NEEDED:

- Anything associated with ears!

| | |
|---|---|
| Earmuffs | Earplugs |
| Earrings | Bell |
| Glasses | Stethoscope |
| Earphones | Ear of corn |
| Cotton Swabs | Phone |
| Headbands | Seashell |
| Hat | |

## DIRECTIONS/OPTIONS:

- Place the "ear" items in different locations throughout the room.
- Have the children go on a "hunt" to find them.
- Have them place the items in a bag or box as they find them.

## GROSS MOTOR:

- **Locomotion:** Instruct the child to retrieve the items utilizing his/her target locomotion goals (e.g., walk, skip, hop, crawl, etc.)
- Place the objects where the child can see them, but in locations that make him or her have to reach, stoop, etc.

## FINE MOTOR:

- Have the child put on or show how to use the objects (e.g., putting on a hat, holding a phone and talking, putting on headphones, etc.)
- **Pincer Grasp:** Have the child utilize grasping skills as he/she reaches for the objects and transfers them to his/her box or bag.
- Trace the objects onto a piece of paper. Have the child match the shapes of the object to the actual object. You can even let the child trace them for you!

# Animal Ears

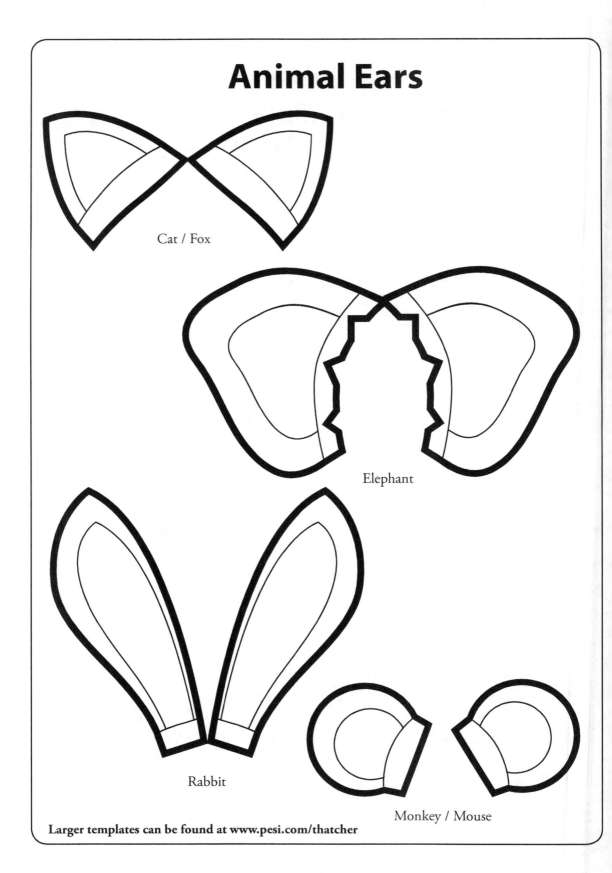

Cat / Fox

Elephant

Rabbit

Monkey / Mouse

# ORAL LANGUAGE:

- Describe an object that you want the child to find. For example, "Find the object that we wear on our head when it is cold outside." Provide the child with the correct word for the object if he/she does not know it (earmuffs, stethoscope, etc.)

- Once the child locates an object, have him/her describe what we do with it, how we use it, who uses it, how it is related to your ears, etc.

- Talk about hearing, the importance of our ears, how we use our hearing, what would happen if we couldn't hear, etc.

- **Phonemic Awareness:** After the child finds the object, have him/her produce the first sound in the word. In addition, have him/her make rhyming words for the object. For example, 'phone' starts with the F sound – it rhymes with stone, moan, loan, cone, etc.

# WRITTEN LANGUAGE:

- Make a map using pictures of the objects. Have the child follow the map to find the objects.

- Write the words of each object on an index card. Have the child place the object next to the word she/he thinks goes with the object. Give clues such as "Stethoscope is a LONG word" or "Glasses start with the letter 'G'." Or, have the child look for letters that he/she recognizes on the index cards.

# SOCIAL/PRAGMATIC:

- Play "telephone" with the children by saying a message to one child and having him/her repeat it to the next child. Each child repeats the sentence to the child sitting beside her/him. The last child in the activity to hear the message says out loud what she/he heard. See how close the message is to the original message. Talk about the importance of listening, how information gets mixed up, what happens when we misunderstand someone, etc.

- Watch a movie without sound. Talk with the children about how it felt to see others talking and not know what they were saying. Talk about people who do not hear well, how they communicate, what causes hearing loss, etc.

- Talk about the importance of communicating with others, when we need to tell adults things, how and when we tell things to other people, etc.

# COGNITIVE:

- Talk about things that make it hard to hear and easy to hear. For example, it's harder to hear when you are wearing earplugs, earmuffs, or have a cold. But when you are wearing a stethoscope, you can hear sounds that are very quiet.

- Have the children talk about noises they like and don't like and categorize them. For example, sounds we like: singing, clapping, bells, birds chirping, Mom's voice. Sounds we don't like: a saw, breaking glass, crying, yelling, etc.
- Have the child line up the objects from smallest to largest.

## SENSORY:

- Place an object such as a hat, earmuffs, earplugs, in or over the child's ears. Make sounds and have the child try to identify the sound and where it came from.

## ACTIVITY 3 — Toss it To and Fro

## MATERIALS NEEDED:

- Large piece of butcher paper or felt
- Ears, nose, mouth, eyes from template page 156
- Glue or tape
- Scissors
- Beanbags
- Chalk, marker, crayon
- Masking tape

## DIRECTIONS/OPTIONS:

- Cut the piece of paper or felt in a large circle.
- Cut the ears, nose, mouth and eyes from the template and tape/glue them on the circle to make a large face.
- You can put numbers on each of the body parts so they each count for different points. For example, ears are worth 5 points, eyes are worth 10, the mouth is worth 15, and the nose is worth 20!
- Place a piece of masking tape on the floor and tell the child to stand behind it. Then have the child toss the beanbags to score as many points as he/she can.
- The child can keep track of his or her points using the chalk, marker, etc.
- Another fun option for score keeping is to make multiple smaller body parts and let the child keep score by tallying the number of times he/she hits the ears, eyes, mouth, etc.

## GROSS MOTOR:

- Instruct the child to throw the beanbags using different standing positions such as standing on two feet, standing on one foot, tossing the beanbags backwards, tossing it between legs, etc.
- Have the child toss the beanbags while sitting on a therapy ball or standing on a rocker board/wobble board.
- Have the child retrieve his/her own beanbags. Work on bending, stooping, etc.

## FINE MOTOR:

- Use different weights of beanbags. Have the child throw them using different types of grips on the beanbags. For example, holding the beanbag in the palm of his/her hand, holding the beanbag using a pincer grip, etc. Have the child throw the beanbags overhand, underhand, backwards over his head, sideways, etc.

## ORAL LANGUAGE:

- Have the child name the body part that he/she is aiming for, then name the part they actually hit. Model a proper sentence for them: "I want to hit the nose," or "I hit the mouth."

- **Concepts:** Tell the child to describe where the beanbag landed. For example, "The bean bag is on the nose," "The beanbag is beside the ear," "I threw it over the face," etc.

- Have the child look in a mirror and describe what she/he looks like. You may need to model what to say by describing what you look like also, or you could ask the child to describe what you look like and you could describe what the child looks like.

- **Phonemic Awareness:** Have the child produce phrases or sentences using alliteration. For example, "I hit a nasty nose,"; "I hit a monkey's mouth,"; "I hit Elmer's ear," etc.

## WRITTEN LANGUAGE:

- Provide different ways for the child to tally her/his score. For example, marking with a straight line every time she/he hits the nose, writing the actual numbers that she/he lands on, or using the smaller body parts for every time she/he lands on one.

## SOCIAL/PRAGMATIC:

- **Sharing and Turn-Taking:** Allow the children to take turns throwing the beanbags. Have each child retrieve the beanbags for another child.

- **Teamwork:** Have the children compete in teams for the largest score. Talk about cheering on teammates, the other team, being a good sport, following the rules of the game, etc.

## COGNITIVE:

- **Counting:** Have the child keep score or you keep the score. Count the number of tally marks, instructing the child to count along with you, or allow the child to count on his/her own.

- **Problem-Solving:** Talk about how the game could be played if there were no beanbags and what else could be used. Also discuss how teams should be set up, what to do if you have trouble hitting a target, etc.

- **Visual Memory:** Place the beanbags on certain areas of the face, allowing the child to watch. Have the child turn around and tell you where the beanbags were placed on the face.

## SENSORY:

- **Tactile Exploration:** Use different items to fill the beanbags (beans, rice, sand, stuffing, Kleenex, cotton balls, beads, paper, macaroni, etc.). Have the child handle and feel the beanbags, describing what each feels like, whether it is heavy or light, etc.

- Correspond the body part the beanbag lands on with a sensory experience. For example, if the beanbag lands on the nose, the child smells a particular scent (perfume, fruit, flower, etc.)

# Ears, Nose, Mouth and Eyes

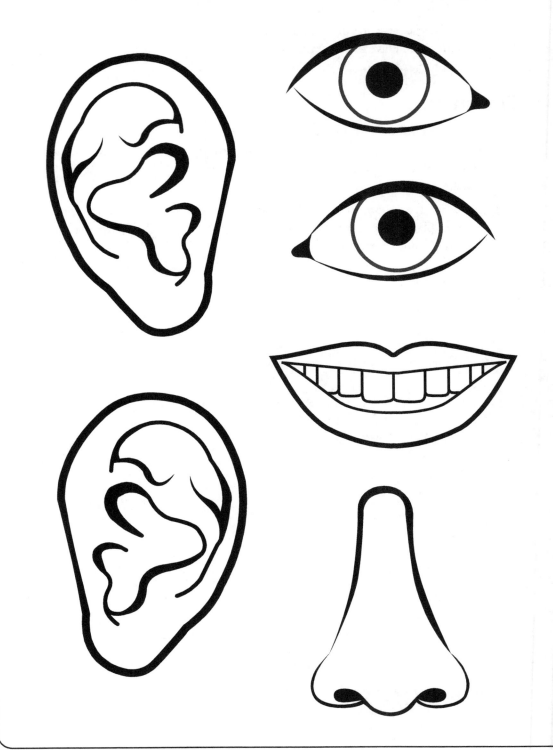

# ACTIVITY 4

# Continental March

## MATERIALS NEEDED:

- Empty paper towel roll
- Scissors
- Hole punch
- Decorative items:
    Glitter
    Paint
    Tinfoil
    Markers
    Sequins
- Yarn or string
- Body parts from template page 156
- Music for marching

## DIRECTIONS/OPTIONS:

- Copy the body parts (ear, nose, mouth, eyes) from the template. Make the parts smaller so that they can be hung from the paper towel roll.
- Allow the child to decorate his/her paper towel roll by painting it, coloring it, rolling it in glitter, or wrapping it in tinfoil.
- Cut the yarn or string in different lengths.
- Using the hole punch, make a small hole in each body part and on one end of the paper towel roll.
- Tie a string through each body part and then tie the other end of the string to the paper towel roll and it becomes a "marching baton!!"
- Have the child hold the marching baton at the bottom (the end without the body parts) and march around the room like a "continental soldier!!"
- March to music or sing the song waving the baton "to and fro."

## GROSS MOTOR:

- **Locomotion:** Have the children march using different types of locomotion such as walking, hopping, jumping, skipping, marching, etc.
- Have the children hold the baton in different positions such as over their heads, beside their legs, swinging it, etc.

## FINE MOTOR:

- **Tying:** Allow the children to tie their own strings if they are able. If the children require assistance, have them do one step of the tying process, for example, allow them to pull the yarn under or over as appropriate.
- Have the children move the baton using wrist rotation, flexion, etc.
- Allow the children to color or paint their baton.

## ORAL LANGUAGE:

- **Following Directions:** Provide verbal directions on where the child should march. For example, "March to the desk and turn around. Now march to the door and open it. March around in a circle," etc.
- **Vocabulary:** Tell the children to name items they see on their march. If they see an item they do not know the name of, provide the proper name of the item.
- Talk about soldiers and what they do. Allow the children to talk about people they know who are soldiers.
- Play "Mother May I March," having the children ask if they can march. Provide them the action and distance they can march. For example, "You can march in three giant hops."
- **Phonemic Awareness:** Instruct the children to march to the beat of the song.

## WRITTEN LANGUAGE:

- **Pre-Literacy:** Have the children use the baton to point to the words on the poster as the song is sung.

## SOCIAL/PRAGMATIC:

- **Turn-Taking:** Instruct the children to march in a line, allowing one child to lead, holding the baton.
- Have the child or children draw pictures or "letters" to send to soldiers. Check around to see if any of the children have a family member who is a soldier and send the notes to that soldier.

## COGNITIVE:

- **Counting:** Tell the children to count the number of steps they are taking as they march.
- **Measuring:** Use a tape measure or yardstick to measure the distance a child can jump, march, hop, etc. Talk about how the distance will be different for each person, why it is longer or shorter, etc.

## SENSORY:

- **Auditory:** March with the music off and tell the children to listen to how their footsteps sound. Have them stomp, tiptoe, slide, etc.

## ACTIVITY 5 — Animal Munch

### MATERIALS NEEDED:

- Tortillas
- Wax paper
- Cream cheese, peanut butter
- Plastic knife
- Raisins
- M&M's®
- Chocolate chips
- Apple slices
- Marshmallows
- Licorice sticks
- Recipe template from page 161 with written ingredients and directions.

### DIRECTIONS:

- Place the tortilla flat on the wax paper.
- Spread a thin layer of either peanut butter or cream cheese on the tortilla.
- Decorate the tortilla to look like a face using the raisins, M&M's etc. (the apple slice makes a great smile!!).
- Eat the parts of the face or roll it up and eat it all at once!!

### GROSS MOTOR:

- **Locomotion:** Place the items for the snack around the room in key locations. Have the children retrieve the items using target locomotion goals. For example, skipping, hopping, climbing, jumping, etc.
- Have the children set out their faces so that others can see them. Move around in various locomotion modes to see what each child made!!

### FINE MOTOR:

- Allow the child to spread peanut butter or cream cheese.
- Have the child use a pincer grasp to pick up and place decorative items on the tortilla. The child can also use tweezers or tongs to pick up items.
- Have the child roll the tortilla before eating it!

## ORAL LANGUAGE:

- **Description:** Ask the child to describe how he or she is making his or her face (e.g., what items is he/she using, how is it being arranged, what items does he/she like to eat, etc.).

- **Requesting Items:** Have the child request the items that she/he needs to complete the snack. You may need to model the verbal requests, such as, "Will you pass the peanut butter?" or "May I have the M&M's?"

- **Basic Concepts:** Compare and contrast the children's faces with yours or another child's. Talk about the concepts of "same" and "different" in regards to colors used, items used, shape, etc.

- **Phonemic Awareness:** Instruct the child to make up rhyming words for each of the items that she/he uses on the face. For example, "cream cheese, peas please, bees sees," etc.

## WRITTEN LANGUAGE:

- **Pre-Literacy:** Spread the peanut butter or cream cheese on some extra tortillas. Allow the child to write letters using his or her fingers in the spread.

- Have the items written out and allow the child to cross off each item of the recipe as he/she uses it.

## SOCIAL/PRAGMATIC:

- **Table Manners:** Talk about using a napkin and table utensils, sharing and passing items to everyone at the table, and how it's not polite to chew with our mouths open.

- **Generalizing/Relating to Experiences:** Tell the child or children to talk about other things that they like/don't like to eat with peanut butter or cream cheese. Also talk about other things we make using tortillas.

## COGNITIVE:

- **Sorting:** Tell the child to sort the decorative items into containers before he/she starts the activity.

- **Colors:** Have the child name or sort M&M's or other items by color.

- **Visual Closure:** Make a tortilla with the face parts missing. The child can identify what it needs to make the face complete!!

## SENSORY:

- **Tactile Exploration:** Allow the child to touch all the decorative items with his/her fingers. Using his/her fingers, the child can smash the M&M's, spread the peanut butter, pull the licorice, squash the marshmallows, etc.

# Animal Munch

**Ingredients:**

_____    _____
_____    _____
_____    _____
_____    _____
_____    _____
_____    _____

**Directions:**

_____
_____
_____
_____
_____
_____
_____
_____
_____
_____
_____
_____
_____
_____
_____
_____
_____

## ACTIVITY 6

# Ears in Mirrors
## (Birth to Three Years of Age)

### MATERIALS NEEDED:

- Large mirror
- Stuffed animals or baby doll
- Bubbles

### DIRECTIONS/OPTIONS:

- Set up a mirror so that you and the child can look in it together (you can sit behind or beside the child).
- Sing the song using the hand gestures or finger plays as suggested. If the child is unable to complete the task independently, assist the child as needed.
- Place the stuffed animals or doll in front of the mirror in a sitting position.
- Use the mirror to find different body parts.

### GROSS MOTOR:

- Practice sitting, crawling, standing, hopping, etc. in front of the mirror as appropriate for the child's current skill level.
- Sing the song or play music and encourage the child to dance in front of the mirror (they can dance with a favorite stuffed animal or doll).
- Place the stuffed animals or dolls in different locations around the room. Tell the child to retrieve them and bring them back in front of the mirror.
- Direct the child to pick up a favorite stuffed animal using anything but his/her hands (e.g., elbows, feet, knees, etc.)

### FINE MOTOR:

- Show the child how to "help" the stuffed animals or doll make the hand movements in the mirror as you sing the song.
- Tell the child to point to his/her different body parts in the mirror or on himself/herself as the song is sung. Or you can name the body parts and ask him/her to point.

- Blow bubbles while sitting in front of the mirror. As the bubbles fall, the child can use his/her fingers, toes, nose etc. to try and touch them!
- Instruct the child to practice taking on and off shoes, socks, coats in front of the mirror.

## ORAL LANGUAGE:

- Ask the child to identify body parts by their function. For example, "Show me what we use to smell; Show me what you use to smile; Show me what you use to walk," etc.
- **Vocabulary:** Tell the child to name body parts. Provide new vocabulary for those children who may not know the parts, such as chin, elbow, wrist, etc.
- Sing other songs that contain body parts, such as This Little Piggy, The Hokey Pokey, Head; Shoulders, Knees and Toes, etc.
- **Phonemic Awareness:** Sing the song with the child as you both move body and hands to the rhythm of the music, or clap the rhythm of the song.

## WRITTEN LANGUAGE:

- **Pre-Literacy:** Read a book to the child in front of the mirror.

## SOCIAL/PRAGMATIC:

- **Emotions:** Make happy, sad, and funny faces in front of the mirror. Talk about what makes us happy, sad, etc. Sing If You're Happy and You Know It.
- Give bear hugs and kisses to the animals. Talk about love, friends, family, etc.
- **Eye Contact:** Encourage the child to make eye contact with you using the mirror.
- Have the child put Band-Aids on different parts of his or her body. Talk about things that can hurt us, telling others when we are hurt, etc.

## COGNITIVE:

- Use the different stuffed animals to compare the size of ears, the number of legs, the length of the legs, what the animals are made of, etc.
- Give the child clothes that are too big or too small for him or her. Let him/her put on the clothes in front of the mirror, talk about how the item fits, whether it's too big or too small, who it does fit, etc.

## SENSORY:

- **Tactile Exploration:** Sing the song and use different textured items (e.g., a feather, wet washcloth, brush, soft blanket, etc.) to rub over different body parts (feet, hand, tummy, back, etc.). Allow the child to watch in the mirror.

# Hickory, Dickory, Dock

Hickory, dickory, dock.
The mouse ran up the clock.
The clock struck one,
The mouse ran down,
Hickory, dickory, dock.

1. Sing the song aloud for child/children.

2. Sing the song again, encouraging child/children to sing along. Use the poster and point to the words in the song as you sing them or allow a child to point for you.

3. Sing the song again and have the child/children participate by voicing and motioning along with you as much as possible. Introduce hand gestures/finger plays to the child/children.

## Suggestions for Hand Motions/Finger Plays:

- Sway side to side as if to imitate a pendulum.
- Sign "mouse" by having your forefinger brush across your nose to represent the twitching nose of a mouse.
- Move your fingers up in a running motion.
- Hold up one finger when you say "one."
- Move your fingers down in a running motion.

# Mouse Maze

## Materials Needed:

- Mouse template from page 173
- Clock template from page 169
- Tape
- Any item that can be used to make a maze:

| | |
|---|---|
| Chairs | Boxes |
| Tables | Hula-Hoop |
| Cones | Balance beam |
| Mat(s) | Bench |
| Rocker board | Seesaw |
| Foam roll and/or wedge | Tunnel |
| Large blocks | Heavy blanket |

## Directions:

- Set up the maze around the room.
- Prepare five mice and one clock by printing/copying the mouse and clock template and the cutting them all out. Add mice as needed to provide an appropriate challenge for each child.
- Place the clock at the end of the maze and the mice throughout the maze.
- Show the child the mouse and instruct him or her to follow the maze to find all the mice you have hidden. Be sure to tell him or her how many mice he/she should be able to find.
- Tell the child to place the mice on the clock at the end of the maze when he/she finishes.

## Gross Motor:

- **Locomotion/Strengthening:** Have the child/children move through the maze. Some options for the maze are:

  Benches to step up on and jump or step off of;
  Jump into/out of a Hula-Hoop;
  Crawl through a tunnel;
  Crawl under a chair;
  Weave in and out of obstacles (cones, cups, large blocks);
  Jump or crawl over a small object (rolled up blanket);

Use a scooter board:
>  Work in a prone position using arms to propel.
>  Work in a sitting position using feet to propel.

# FINE MOTOR:

- **Manipulation/Dexterity:** Attach the mice to different objects using different modes of fastening (tape, paper clips, clothes pins, Velcro, etc.). The children remove each of the mice and then must reattach them to the clock in the same manner.

- **Scissor Skills:** Allow each child to cut out his/her own mice and clock.

# ORAL LANGUAGE:

- **Oral Expression:** Play Mother May I while going through the maze. For example, "May I jump over the blanket? May I crawl under the chair? May I slide under the bench?" etc.

- **Vocabulary:** Talk about words the children may not know such as maze, hickory, dickory, dock (a play on words), etc. Talk about other words that mean the same as maze.

- **Description:** Have the child describe the actions, prepositions, objects, etc. as he/she manipulates the maze. Provide additional details as the child verbalizes his/her descriptions.

- **Phonemic Awareness:** Have the child substitute words that rhyme in the song. For example, "Hickory, dickory, dock, the mouse ran up the *sock*, the *sock* struck *gong*, the mouse ran down, hickory, dickory dock." You may need to model rhyming words and have the child sing along with you.

# WRITTEN LANGUAGE:

- Write letters or short words on the front of each mouse. See if the child recognizes any of the letters or words.

- Give the child a letter at the beginning of the maze and tell him/her to find only the mice with that letter on them.

# SOCIAL/PRAGMATIC:

- **Teamwork:** Have the children complete the maze in teams of two. Stress the importance of working together to complete each task and find all of the mice.

- **Generalizing/Relating to Experiences:** Talk about a time that the child may have been lost or with their parents when they were lost. Talk about how a store can seem like a maze if a child is separated from parents or a caregiver. Talk about how the child felt and how the problem was solved.

## COGNITIVE:

- **Colors:** Make the mice different colors. When the child completes the maze, have him/her find only a certain color of mouse; or, he/she can find all the yellow mice first, then the red mice, then the green mice, etc.

- **Counting:** Count the number of mice as the child places them on the clock and have the child count along with you.

- **Following Directions:** Have the child put the mice back as she/he goes through the maze (tell her/him where to place them, for example, "Put the mouse under the chair"; "Put the mouse in the box," etc.)

## SENSORY:

- **Tactile Exploration:** Set up the maze to provide a sensory experience: Have the child search for a mouse submerged in beans or rice.

# Clock

## ACTIVITY 2 — Number Hunt

### MATERIALS NEEDED:

- Small brown paper bag
- Clock template on page 169
- Glue or tape
- Scissors
- Crayons, paint, markers
- Anything with numbers!!

| | |
|---|---|
| Labels | Books |
| Calendars | Computer keyboard |
| Phone | Clocks |
| Remote control | Number line or chart |
| Magnetic plastic numbers | Shirts or jerseys |
| Mice templates from page 173 with numbers on them | Room numbers (signs on doors) |

### DIRECTIONS:

- Copy the clock template and glue or tape it on the side of a brown paper bag.
- Copy multiple mice from the template and write a number on each one.
- Allow the child to cut out the clock and mice if he/she is able.
- Have the child decorate the bag by writing numbers all over it and the clock, which is attached to one side of the bag.
- Place items around the room that have numbers on them, such as the mice, plastic magnetic numbers, etc.
- Have the child find items with numbers on them around the room. Put the item in the bag if it will fit.

### GROSS MOTOR:

- **Locomotion:** Have the children go on their "hunt" using different modes of locomotion. You may have them walk, crawl, skip, hop, jump, etc.
- Put the items at different heights throughout the classroom. Encourage the children to squat to look under furniture or jump to see if there is something up high above their heads. You may also have some items that the child must move

in order to find an object, for example, having to move a chair out of the way to reach a numbered mouse.

## FINE MOTOR:

- Have the child cut out the clock, glue or tape it onto a bag, and decorate the bag.

- After the child locates a number, tell him/her to bring it to you and he/she can perform one of the following options based on the materials/equipment available to you:

  Attach a mouse to a bulletin board using a pushpin *(with close supervision)*
  Attach the mouse or magnetic letters to a dry erase board, magnetic board, or metal furniture.

- Have the child use a pincer grasp to retrieve and place items in the bag. He/she can also take items out of the bag.

## ORAL LANGUAGE:

- Talk about all the things the children find with numbers on them. Ask various questions, such as what does each item do, how are the numbers used, how many numbers are on each, etc.

- Have the children brainstorm on what items they could be looking for that might have numbers on them before beginning the hunt. If the children cannot think of any items, take them on a walk and show them examples of some.

- **Phonemic Awareness:** Have the children think of words that rhyme with the numbers 1-10. Have them list as many words as they can think of that rhyme with each number.

- **Phonemic Awareness:** Have the children clap out words that fit one beat, two beats, three beats, etc. by clapping out the syllables in the words. Talk about how longer words will have more claps, and shorter words might only have one clap.

- **Concepts:** Talk about concepts such as up/down, under/over, etc. Where did the child find the items (on the wall, up high, down low, etc.). Talk about number concepts such as many, few, more, etc.

## Written Language:

- **Pre-Literacy:** Make a list of all items you can find with numbers on them. Have the child cross them off as she/he finds them.

- **Number Formulation:** Have the children trace different numbers that they find with their fingers. You can also have them practice writing their own numbers if they are able to!

## Social/Pragmatic:

- **Time Perception:** Talk with the children about time, the concept of a daily schedule (e.g., when school starts, what time to have a snack, what time a favorite show starts, being on time, how people use watches/clocks to know what time it is, night time/day time, etc.)

- **Consequences:** Talk about how important it is that a society use clocks and time. What would happen if no one knew what time to be to work, what time stores open or close, what time to take medicine, what time a sporting event starts, etc.

## Cognitive:

- **Counting and Number Concepts:** Have the children count items (M&M's, manipulatives, chips, blocks, etc.) to match each number. For example, they could use one block for #1, 2 blocks for #2, 3 blocks for #3, etc.

- Instruct the children to try and put the numbers on the clock in the correct order. If a child is not able to complete this independently, go ahead and put most of the numbers in order, leaving out one or two so they can find the correct placement.

## Sensory:

- **Tactile Exploration:** Have the children feel and describe the texture, weight, etc. of each of the items they find with numbers. Ask them if they can feel the numbers on each item, such as a sign, calendar, phone, or not feel the numbers on items such as the clock.

- **Auditory:** Place a loud ticking clock somewhere in the room. Instruct the child or children to listen closely to try and find where the ticking noise is coming from. Or use a clock with an alarm, and when the alarm sounds, the kids look for the clock!!

# Mice

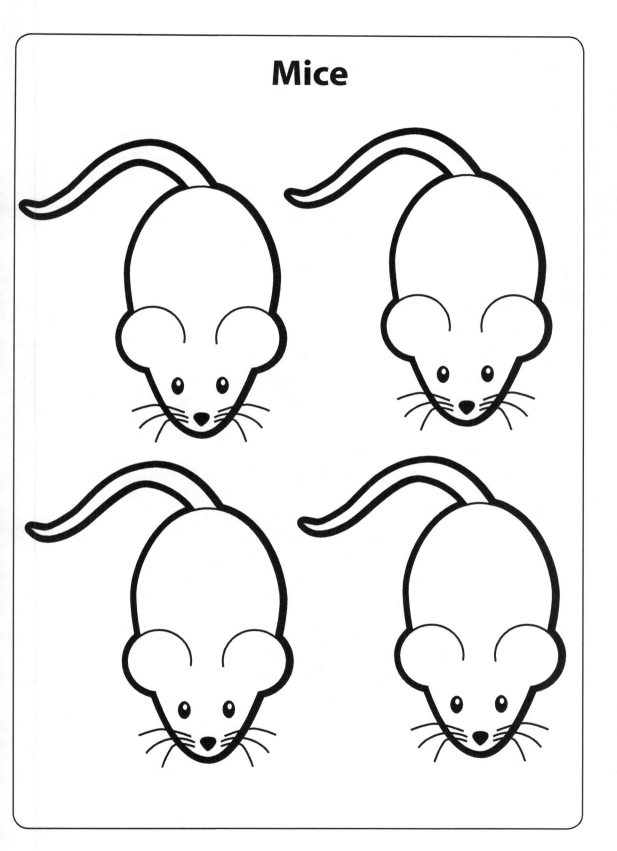

# Rock 'N' Mouse

## MATERIALS NEEDED:

- Small/medium rock
- Glue
- Yarn
- Paint
- Scissors
- Felt
- Pipe Cleaners

## DIRECTIONS:

- Find a nice smooth oval rock.
- Wash the rock with soap and water and dry it thoroughly.
- Cut small triangle shapes from felt for ears.
- Cut small strips from felt for whiskers (or use pipe cleaners).
- Paint eyes, a nose and mouth on one end of the rock.
- Glue a tail on the other end of the rock.
- Glue whiskers around the mouth.

## GROSS MOTOR:

- **Locomotion:** Go outside and find the "perfect" rock. Encourage the child to look in obscure places or places where she/he may need to crawl, etc. Allow the child to pick out several rocks, putting them in one central location. Then have the child choose the one rock she/he wants. Instruct the child to replace all the other rocks that were not chosen.

- After the mouse is completed, allow the child to make the mouse move around on the floor. Or have the "mouse" chase other "mice."

- Have the child move like a mouse. He/she can run, scamper, creep, etc. Ask the child which one takes more time.

## FINE MOTOR:

- **Scissor Skills:** Allow the child to cut the tail and small pieces for the ears. Remember, they don't need to be perfect. Individual differences in the materials make individual mice!!

- Have the child paint his/her rocks grey or other fun colors. If the child is able, allow him/her to paint the eyes, nose, and mouth using either a paintbrush or cotton swab.

- **Pincer Grasp:** Have the child put a small amount of glue on the rock for a tail and whiskers using a cotton swab. Then have the child place the tail and whiskers on the rock and hold them until they dry.

## ORAL LANGUAGE:

- **Vocabulary:** Talk about mice, where they live, what they eat, how they move (e.g., by creeping, scampering, running, etc.), mice as pets/wild mice, what mice look like, have you ever seen a mouse, etc.

- Talk about famous mice (Mickey and Minnie Mouse, Mighty Mouse, Stuart Little) and famous cats (Garfield, Hello Kitty, Felix, Morris).

- **Concepts:** Have the child/children place their mice in different locations throughout the room (on the chair, under the table, high on a counter, inside a box, beside the desk, etc.). Have them describe where they placed their mice, or provide verbal directions of where to place the mice and have the children follow your directions.

- **Phonemic Awareness:** Sing other songs about mice or cats such as Three Blind Mice and Three Little Kittens. Have the child or children move to the different rhythms of the songs.

## WRITTEN LANGUAGE:

- **Pre-Literacy:** Talk about the letters in the words 'cat' and 'mouse'. Use the paint to write the words on index cards. Have the children find letters they recognize, count how many letters are in each word, etc. The children can also trace the letters with their fingers or have their "mouse" run over the letters.

## SOCIAL/PRAGMATIC:

- Talk about the relationship between cats and mice and how they don't get along. Also discuss how sometimes people don't get along, how to get along with people we may not agree with, why some people don't like others, etc.

- Talk about being scared of things (like mice!!) and how different people are afraid of different things. Talk about how we react to things we are afraid of.

## COGNITIVE:

- **Visual Closure:** Position the mice around the room, partially hidden to obstruct them from the children's view as they look for them.

- **Generalizing:** Instruct the children to brainstorm on what other animals could be made from rocks (turtles, cats, rabbits, etc.). Let them make another rock animal to be a friend to their mouse!!

## SENSORY:

- **Tactile Exploration:** Find different rocks with different surface textures, shapes, sizes, etc. Allow the children to investigate the rocks in various states, such as when they are wet, warm/cold, dirty, etc.

## ACTIVITY 4

# Color-by-Number
# Mouse and Clock

## MATERIALS NEEDED:

- Color-by-Number template on page 179
- Crayons or markers

## DIRECTIONS:

- Copy the Color-by-Number mouse and clock template.
- Enlarge it as needed for the needs of the child.
- Follow the numbers/colors to make your own miniature 'Hickory, Dickory, Dock' poster.

## GROSS MOTOR:

- **Locomotion:** Instruct the child to do the actions associated with the song after he/she finishes coloring her/his poster (e.g., swinging like a pendulum, jumping up like the mouse running up the clock, etc.)
- **Core/Proximal Shoulder Strengthening:** Tape the picture on the wall and have the child color against the wall.

## FINE MOTOR:

- **Visual-Motor/Pre-Handwriting Skills:** Have the child color the picture using vertical, horizontal, or circular strokes/scribbles. Choose a direction that will present an appropriate challenge.

## ORAL LANGUAGE:

- Talk about the picture before beginning to color. See if the child can guess what the picture is, what colors might be used, how to use the numbers to see what colors to use, etc.
- Talk about the colors being used and the different names for colors (violet/purple, red/maroon, forest green, etc.). Other things you could talk about with the child are his/her favorite color, the color of his/her room, what color shirt she/he has on, etc. Find different colors in the room that match the colors being used in the picture.

- Talk about how even when the pictures and directions are the same, pictures can look different. For example, coloring darker/lighter, using different shades of colors, etc.

- **Phonemic Awareness:** After the picture is finished, sing the song and have the child follow along with the words on her/his picture as you point on the poster.

## WRITTEN LANGUAGE:

- **Pre-Literacy:** Have the child find the names of colors on the crayons. Instruct him/her to practice writing the name of the color using that color crayon (blue, red, green, orange, etc.)

## SOCIAL/PRAGMATIC:

- **Sharing:** Since everyone will need the same colors, instruct the children to practice sharing the colors. Talk with them about ways they can share (e.g., one child using red to color all the red areas while another child uses blue).

- Hang all the pictures and have the children talk about how they are different or the same, which ones they like, and ask each child to describe his/her own picture, etc.

## COGNITIVE:

- Talk about using the numbers as a guide or map to coloring the picture, how the children can start with number one and do all of that number before moving on to different numbers and colors, etc.

- Partially color a picture and have the children identify which areas still need to be colored. Ask them what number on the picture has been colored and what color corresponds to it, etc.

## SENSORY:

- Practice pressing hard and easy with the crayons. Ask the children how the colors look different if they press hard or soft on the crayons.

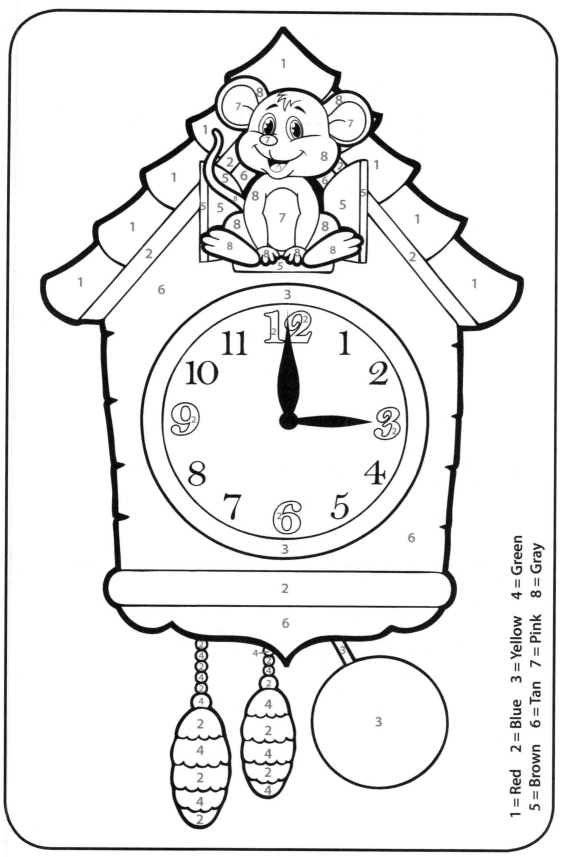

# Mouse's Cheese

## MATERIALS NEEDED:

- Several types of cheese
- Toothpicks
- Foods to eat with cheese:

  | | |
  |---|---|
  | Crackers | Apples |
  | Pears | Peaches |
  | Grapes | Lunch meat |
  | Tomatoes | Bread |

## DIRECTIONS:

- Use either sliced or cubed cheese.
- If using crackers or bread, sliced cheese works best.
- If you use cubed cheese, use the toothpicks to skewer the cheese and alternate with other foods such as the grapes, meat, or tomatoes.

## GROSS MOTOR:

- Encourage the children to be on "a hunt for cheese." Have them "scamper" throughout the room to find the items for the snack. They can move using various modes of locomotion as appropriate for their goals.
- Have the children sit on balance balls/therapy balls to prepare the snack.

## FINE MOTOR:

- Have the children practice sticking the toothpick into the food items and use a pincer grasp to pick up the items to eat.
- Have the child roll up various food items in a slice of cheese.
- Encourage the child to take "tiny mouse bites" of cheese (like a mouse). She/he can also practice tearing off small pieces of crackers to make them the right size for a mouse.

# ORAL LANGUAGE:

- Talk about what mice eat (cheese!), how they find it, why mice like it, how they eat it, how they carry it back to their home, and what other things besides cheese mice eat.

- Describe what the different types of cheese look like. Why are they different colors, why do some have holes (i.e., Swiss), why some is round vs, square, etc. Other questions to ask: What is cheese made of?; What animal(s) does cheese come from?

- Talk about how we get or make the other food items in the snack. For example, we grow apples, grapes, and other fruit, we make crackers from flour, etc.

- **Phonemic Awareness:** Think of rhyming words for each of the ingredients in the snack. For example, apple/dapple, rapple/Snapple, etc.

# WRITTEN LANGUAGE:

- **Labels:** Have the children look at the labels on the cheese packages to find letters and numbers they might recognize.

- Use the toothpicks to make letters and numbers.

# SOCIAL/PRAGMATIC:

- Talk about how all animals and living things need food to survive. How do different animals find their food, prepare their food, what types of food do different animals like, etc.

- Talk about healthy food. This is a good time to show the food pyramid and the different types of food we need to stay healthy. Ask the children how eating healthy makes you feel better and grow healthy.

# COGNITIVE:

- **Patterning:** Have the child create a pattern of food on the toothpick (e.g., cheese-grape-meat, or give them a pattern such as fruit-cheese-fruit and let them decide which fruits to use).

- **Generalizing:** Have the children think of other food items with the word 'cheese' in it (e.g., cheese puffs, cream cheese, cheese nips, cheese ball, etc.). Ask if these are the same kind of cheese they just ate, how is it different, etc.

- **Counting:** Stick several toothpicks in a piece of cheese and have the child pull them out and count them.

# SENSORY:

- **Oral Exploration:** Talk about the different textures of the foods in the activity. Have the child think of words to describe each texture as he tastes it. For example, crackers are crunchy, the cheese is soft, the lunch meat is cold and slimy, etc.

## ACTIVITY 6

# Quiet as a Mouse
## (Birth to Three Years of Age)

### MATERIALS NEEDED:

- Canisters or bottles (with lids!)
- Filler materials:

| | |
|---|---|
| Cereal | Pretzels |
| Cotton balls | Crumpled paper |
| Coins | Rice |
| Instant potatoes | Small pebbles |
| Sand | Beads |
| Buttons | Water |
| Dry oats | |

### DIRECTIONS/OPTIONS:

- Fill containers that the child can hold with the different filler materials.
- Make sure the lids are put on tight.
- Shake the different containers as you sing 'Hickory, Dickory, Dock'.

### GROSS MOTOR:

- Have the child/children shake the container in different positions. For example, have them shake the container by rolling it from side to side on the ground, jumping up and down with the container, shaking it while laying on their backs, while balancing on a ball, etc.

### FINE MOTOR:

- Use a container that the child can open and close himself. Allow him/her to open it to put in new items.
- The child could scoop items into the container to practice forearm rotation. He/she could also dip the container into the filler item to fill it up.
- Place the container where the child will have to cross midline to grasp it.

# Oral Language:

- **Concepts:** Talk with the child about the concepts of loud and quiet. Encourage the child to vocalize with any parts of 'Hickory, Dickory, Dock'. Sing the song both loudly and quietly. You can also talk about concepts such as "up" and "down" as the mouse goes up the clock and comes back down.

- **Rhythm, Prosody, Phonemic Awareness:** Sing the song, emphasizing the pitch and intonation changes. Move the child's arms or legs to the rhythm of the song.

- Sing the song, leaving off some key words. Encourage the child to complete the phrase of the song. For example, "Hickory, Dickory, _____."

- Take a walk around the room or outside and talk about the different sounds you hear, where they are coming from, what/who is making it, whether it is loud or soft, whether we hear it only outside or inside, etc.

# Written Language:

- Look through books that contain different animals such as mice, cats, dogs, horses, etc. Name the animals, make the animal noises, move like the animal, etc.

# Social/Pragmatic:

- Talk about noises that may frighten the child (dogs barking, sirens, screams, vacuums, etc.)

- Talk about "inside" and "outside" voices and when to use each. What happens when we use an "outside" voice where we should be using a quiet voice?

# Sensory:

- Use different filler items such as rice, small rocks, beads, etc. and shake the container in various places around the child to provide practice with localizing sounds.

- Allow the child to feel the filler items. Talk about whether the items make noise when touched or moved (paper, oats, etc.)

# Oh Where, Oh Where, Has My Little Dog Gone?

Oh where, oh where, has my little dog gone?
Oh where, oh where could he be?
With his ears cut short and his tail cut long,
Oh where, oh where could he be?

## Suggestions for Hand Motions/Finger Plays:

- Put your hands up in the air as if asking "where" the dog is.
- Pat your lap and snap your fingers as if calling for a dog.
- Grab both your ears.
- Place your hand behind you as if wagging your tail.

## ACTIVITY 1

# Dog Catcher

## Materials Needed:

- Dogs from template on page 189.
- Anything that can be used as a net:
    - Actual bug net
    - Sack
    - Laundry bag
- Tape
- Scissors
- Hat
- Anything that can be used as a cage:
    - Upside-down laundry basket
    - Box
    - Actual cage or crate

## Directions:

- Copy and cut out several dogs from the template.
- Place the dog templates on objects around the room or tape them in different locations in room.
- Allow the child/children to be the "dog catcher" (let her/him wear the official dog catching hat!) finding as many dogs as he/she can and putting them in his/her net.
- Have the child put the dogs in the cage.
- For a variation, put numbers or letters on the dogs, or make dog tags for each one.

## Gross Motor:

- **Locomotion:** Provide instructions on the different types of locomotion for the child as he/she catches the dogs. For example: Walk fast, walk slow, skip, walk backwards, hop, jump, crawl, etc. Place the dogs at various heights.
- Practice the movements needed to swing the net (over the head, etc.)
- Take turns being the dog and the dog catcher. The dog crawls around on the floor barking and the dog catcher uses various modes of locomotion to catch the dog.

# FINE MOTOR:

- Have the child/children color the dogs before putting the dogs out in the room or after they find the dogs.

- Place the dogs on objects using various means (tape, magnets, paper clips, clothes pins, etc.). Once the child finds all the dogs, have him replace all the dogs he found.

# ORAL LANGUAGE:

- **"Wh" Questions:** Talk about the concept of "where" objects or people are in the room. Provide a verbal model of asking "wh" questions and have the child come up with his/her own "wh" questions.

- **Listening:** Cue the child or children to listen closely, before beginning the hunt. Then provide very specific directions before beginning the hunt for the dogs, such as "Find all the brown dogs first" or "Every time you hear a bark, stop!"

- **Concept Development:** Have the child verbalize where he/she found the dogs. For example, "I found a dog on the wall"; "I caught a dog under the table," etc. You could also provide similar cues to help the child catch dogs. For example, "I see a dog by something blue"; "I see a dog beside the window," etc.

- **Phonemic Awareness:** Practice making rhymes for the words of the song. For example, "dog–log, bog-mog-pog"; "gone-don, pawn-dawn-lawn"; "tail–bail, snail-pail-mail," etc.

# WRITTEN LANGUAGE:

- **Pre-Literacy:** Write letters on the each of the dogs' name tags. Provide the child a letter before he/she starts the dog hunt and have him/her attempt to find the letter that it matches.

- **Pre-Literacy:** Write each child's name on a dog tag and have each child locate the dog with his/her name on it.

- Have the child or children make a "lost dog" poster. He/she can draw a picture of the dog and write down a phone number and description of the dog.

# SOCIAL/PRAGMATIC:

- Talk with the children about being responsible for our pets, specifically, making sure our pets have name tags, are fed and watered, that they get the medical care and shots they need, etc.

- Talk about what would happen if a dog or cat got lost and did not have a name tag: Where does the animal go if someone finds him? How do the owners try to find the dog? etc.

## COGNITIVE:

- **Counting:** Have the child keep count of how many dogs he/she has in his/her net. Then have her/him recount the dogs as he/she puts them in the cage.

- **Patterning:** Have the child pattern the dogs by their color, the numbers on the dogs, the letters on the dogs, etc.

## SENSORY:

- **Auditory Stimulation:** Bark loudly as the child gets close to finding a dog, and softer as she/he gets farther away. Talk about how you can use your ears to help you look for the lost dogs.

# Dogs

# ACTIVITY 2

# Paw Print
## Clues

## MATERIALS NEEDED:

- Paw print and bone templates from page 192
- Crayons/markers
- Scissors

## DIRECTIONS/OPTIONS:

- Copy the templates.
- Cut out the templates.
- Arrange the paw prints so that they make a path that the child can follow in order to find the bone at the end of the path! Instruct the children to follow the "clues" to find the bone (or even a stuffed dog at the end!).

## GROSS MOTOR:

- Have the child use various forms of locomotion to follow the paw prints. For example, he could crawl, hop, skip, walk, crab-walk, etc.
- Have the child make his own path with the paw prints, squatting down low to place each print on the floor.
- Go outside and allow the child to dig a hole and bury the bone!

## FINE MOTOR:

- Allow the child to decorate the paw prints/bones before cutting them out.
- **Scissor Skills:** If appropriate, allow the child to cut out the paw prints or the bones for the activity.
- **Pincer Grasp:** Have the child pick up the paw prints as she/he finds them, using a pincer grasp.

# ORAL LANGUAGE:

- Don't show the children the bone, and have them make predications about what they will find at the end of the "trail." When they find the bone, have them discuss whether it was what they predicted, or how it was the same or different.

- Have the child hide the bone and give you clues about where it is located within the room. You may need to hide the bone first and provide a model for verbal clues.

- Talk about why dogs hide bones by digging holes and putting them in the ground, how they find other bones that have been buried (by smell), whether it is safe for dogs to chew on bones, etc.

- **Phonemic Awareness:** Put pictures (dog, cat, doghouse, leash, collar, bone, ball, etc.) on the paw prints. As the child steps on each paw, have her/him make up rhyming words or words that start with the same letter.

# WRITTEN LANGUAGE:

- Look at boxes and bags of pet food. Some questions to ask the children: How can we tell what animal the food is for? What type of information do we find on the container? etc.

# SOCIAL/PRAGMATIC:

- Have the child talk about a time that she/he lost something. How did she/he find it? How did she/he know where to look? Were there any clues to help him/her locate the lost item?

- **Problem-Solving:** Talk with the child about the strategy of "retracing your footsteps" and how that can help you to find something that you lost.

# COGNITIVE:

- **Counting:** Have the child count the paw prints as he/she finds them. Discuss the relationship between the number of paw prints he/she reaches and the length of the trail.

- **Visual Closure:** Place the paw prints/bone so that they are partially obstructed from the child's view, requiring the child to differentiate between the objects and the background.

# SENSORY:

- Talk about how dogs have an amazing sense of smell. Share with the children that dogs might look for the bone using their nose rather than their eyes! Ask the children if they can smell anything in the room, or if they think that they could find items using their sense of smell?

# Paw Prints & Bone

## ACTIVITY 3 — My Puppy Puppet

**ACTIVITY 3**

# My Puppy
## Puppet

## MATERIALS NEEDED:

- Small brown paper bag
- Scissors
- Crayons, markers, paint
- Glue, stapler
- Anything to decorate puppy:
  - Construction paper
  - Furry cloth
  - Yarn
  - Buttons
  - Ribbon for a collar
  - Felt
  - Socks (make great floppy ears!!)
  - Pom-poms
  - Crepe paper

## DIRECTIONS:

- Use the brown paper bag as the puppy's body.
- Use various items to decorate the puppy (for example, cutting small round pieces of black and white construction paper to make the dog a Dalmatian, or cutting lots of black yarn and gluing it all over the bag to make a Scottie).
- Use any items to make the nose and eyes, such as piece of pink or black construction paper, pom-poms, buttons, etc.
- Glue a long, oval piece of red or pink construction paper under the flap of the sack to make a tongue sticking out.
- The tail can be yarn, crepe paper, construction paper, etc.
- Glue a strip of ribbon around the brown paper bag, under the dog's head for a collar.
- Use a small piece of yellow or any color to make a name tag for the puppy and glue it to its collar.

## GROSS MOTOR:

- **Locomotion:** After the child finishes her/his puppy, let him/her take the puppy around the room using developmentally appropriate forms of locomotion.

Or, sing "Oh Where, Oh Where, Has My Little Dog Gone?" and have the child act out their puppy finding "where the little dog has gone."

- Have the child complete the activity while balancing on a therapy ball.

- Take a walk outside and have the child use the puppy puppet to find other animals that we see outside. Look for different types of dogs.

## Fine Motor:

- **Scissor Skills:** Allow the child to cut as many of the puppy parts that he/she is able.

- **Pincer Grasp:** Have the child use a pincer grip to pick up puppy parts from the container or on the table and glue them to the paper bag.

- After the puppy is completed, show the child how to put it over his/her hand to make the puppet talk and move!

## Oral Language:

- After the puppy is completed, tell the child to make it bark or even talk! The children can use the puppy puppet to have a conversation with her/his puppy. The puppy can also sing along with you as you sing the song.

- Talk about all the various types of dogs and how different they look (their different colors, how some have spots, how some are big or little, how some have long ears and tails and some have short ears and tails), how they may have different sounding barks, where dogs might live (inside/outside), etc.)

- Brainstorm all the different names that a puppy could have (Spot, Jack, Bailey, Rex, Chip, Fido, Buster, etc.). How do people name their dogs (by their color, by girl or boy names, etc.)?

- Have the child describe how he/she decorated his/her puppy. Does the puppy puppet look like a puppy he/she has seen before?

- **Phonemic Awareness:** Write all the possible names for the puppies that the child came up with and then make rhyming words for each, or bark the number of syllables in each!

## Written Language:

- **Pre-Literacy:** Look through magazines and books to try and find pictures of different types of dogs.

- Have the child write the name of the dog on the tag or copy it if he/she does not know the word.

## SOCIAL/PRAGMATIC:

- Talk about how the puppy needs help because it is a baby dog. How do we take care of puppies, what do they need, what do they like to play with, etc. Ask how our parents took care of us when we were babies and how they take care of us now that we are growing up.

- Talk about being responsible for animals when they are little: What are some of the jobs a child can do to take care of a puppy (walk him, help feed him, play with him)?

## COGNITIVE:

- Talk about different concepts related to age, such as what it means to be a baby, child, adult, younger/older, etc. Discuss the difference between being a parent and being a child.

- **Visual Closure:** Make your own puppy, leaving off some of the parts. Have the child identify what else the puppy needs.

## SENSORY:

- Instruct the children to bark like dogs using different types of barks (woofs, yips, barks, growls) and different volumes.

# Doggie Dish

## MATERIALS NEEDED:

- Container to make a "dog bowl":
    Cool Whip® container (cleaned out)
    Plastic bowl (even a real dog bowl)
    Styrofoam bowl
- Paint
- Templates of bones and paw prints from pages 192
- Glue
- Scissors
- Markers/crayons
- Plain paper or construction paper

## DIRECTIONS/OPTIONS:

- Decorate the bowl however you wish. You may need to cover any existing writing on the container with construction paper before you begin.
- You can paint the bowl with a design, or color and cut out templates to glue onto the bowl in order to design it.

## GROSS MOTOR:

- Have the child crawl around the room pretending to be a dog. He/she can even pretend to eat out of the bowl.
- **Balance:** Put objects (marbles, wrapped hard candy, etc.) in the bowl. Have the child walk in a straight line while holding the bowl. You can also make a straight line on the floor out of masking tape and have the child walk on it like a balance beam! Have the child stand on a balance board while holding the bowl for another balance activity.
- Have the child make the project while sitting on a balance ball/therapy ball.

## FINE MOTOR:

- Have the child hold the paint brush/crayons/markers appropriately while decorating the bowl.
- **Scissor Skills:** If appropriate, allow the child to cut out the paw prints or the bones for the activity.

# ORAL LANGUAGE:

- **Vocabulary:** Have the child think of as many different types of dishes and silverware as he/she can (e.g., bowls, plates, cups, spoons, knives, etc.). You can also think of more obscure kitchen items, such as a colander, apple corer, etc. and teach the children the names and functions of each one.

- Have the children describe how they decided to decorate their bowls. Have them state what mediums, supplies, and colors they used. Have the children talk about how each of their bowls ended up being different or the same.

- Have the child tell a story about a dog, giving them key vocabulary words to include such as bowl, food, water, bone, hungry, eat, play, sleep, puppy, catch, fetch, etc.

- **Phonemic Awareness:** Have the child or children play the name game with alliteration by saying phrases such as, "My dog's name is Rowdy Rex"; "My dog's name is Joyful Jack"; "My dog's name is Pretty Penny," etc.

# WRITTEN LANGUAGE:

- Help the children write their names on their bowls or a name that they choose for an imaginary or real dog that the bowl could belong to.

# SOCIAL/PRAGMATIC:

- Talk with the children about how a dog eats and drinks out of a bowl on the floor. How is this different from when the children eat a meal with their family? Talk about how people sit at a table, use silverware and napkins, etc.

- Talk about how we know when dogs are hungry or thirsty: What do we need to do when we leave pets at home to make sure they have enough to eat? What happens if pets are left outside when it is very hot or cold?

# COGNITIVE:

- **Visual Memory/Tracking:** Play the "bone game" with 2 or 3 dog bowls. Hide a dog bone under one of the bowls, then mix the bowls around, letting the child watch. See if the child can find the bone!!

- Fill up several dog bowls with different amounts of water, cereal, marbles, etc. Have the child sort the amounts from least to most or most to least.

# SENSORY:

- **Tactile Exploration:** Fill the bowls with different types of items with various textures (e.g., water, rice, uncooked oats, marbles, cotton balls, etc.). Have the child manipulate the items using his or her fingers and hands. Try blindfolding the child to see if he/she can describe or identify the items.

# Puppy Chow

## MATERIALS NEEDED:

- Recipe template from page 201 with written ingredients and directions
- A large bowl
- Small bowls (one for each ingredient)
- Scoops or measuring cups
- Spoons
- At least two of the following (or any good small snack foods) to make "puppy chow":
  - M&Ms®
  - Cereal (Honey Nut Cheerios®, Chex®, Honey Grahams®, etc.)
  - Raisins
  - Marshmallows
  - Chocolate or peanut butter chips
  - Honey roasted peanuts

## DIRECTIONS:

- Place each of the ingredients into separate small bowls or containers.
- Have the child systematically combine the ingredients in the large bowl.
- Have the child stir the ingredients together using a spoon.
- Have the child use a clean cup to scoop out a serving for him or herself.

## GROSS MOTOR:

- **Balance:** Have the child stand on a rocker board/wobble board or sit on a t-stool/therapy ball.
- **Core/Shoulder Strengthening:** Instruct the child to stand or sit up tall as he or she prepares the "puppy chow." The child will be activating/working his or her core muscles while stirring the ingredients.

# FINE MOTOR:

- **Forearm Rotation:** Instruct the child to use scoops or measuring cups to scoop the ingredients out of the small bowls and dump them into the large bowl.

- **Self-Feeding:** Have the child use a spoon to transfer the ingredients from the small bowls to the large bowl. This technique will also address forearm rotation and fine motor dexterity.

- **Pincer Grasp:** As the child eats the snack, cue him or her to pick up one piece at a time using a pincer grasp. If the child does not eat the snack, have him or her release one piece at a time into a bowl to "feed the puppy."

# ORAL LANGUAGE:

- Talk about what real dog food looks like: How is it the same or different than the "puppy chow" we made? Talk about why real dogs should not eat our "puppy chow" because it could make the dog sick.

- **Vocabulary:** Name all the items as the child adds them to the mixture. Also describe the action verbs, such as pouring, stirring, mixing, adding, etc.

- **Describing:** Tell the child to describe the packages that the items come in, such as the box of cereal, the bag of chocolate chips, etc.

- **Phonemic Awareness:** Clap the syllables of all the ingredients (e.g., rai-sin, choco-late, etc.)

# WRITTEN LANGUAGE:

- Write the directions on the following recipe template. Have the child cross off each ingredient as he/she adds it to the mixture.

- Check the packages of the ingredients to see if they have recipes on them.

# SOCIAL/PRAGMATIC:

- **Turn-Taking:** Allow each child to add an ingredient and stir the mixture. He/she can also take turns dipping out "puppy chow" for him/herself.

- **Sharing:** Instruct each child to dip out the "puppy chow" and put it in a sandwich bag to share with others.

## COGNITIVE:

- **Counting:** Have the child count the ingredients used in the recipe or count individual ingredients as he/she adds it to the "puppy chow."

- **Patterning:** Have the child follow or make his/her own pattern using the ingredients. For example: chocolate chip-raisin-Chex, chocolate chip-raisin-Chex, etc.

- **Memory:** Have the child name the ingredients in the order they were added to the mixture.

## SENSORY:

- **Tactile Exploration:** Allow the child to handle the ingredients with his or her fingers. Talk about how each ingredient feels.

- **Taste Exploration:** While eating the "puppy chow," talk about the different ingredients (how they taste, how they feel in the mouth, what noise they make when you chew on them, etc.)

# Puppy Chow

**Ingredients:**

_____     _____
_____     _____
_____     _____
_____     _____
_____     _____
_____

**Directions:**

_____
_____
_____
_____
_____
_____
_____
_____
_____
_____
_____
_____
_____
_____
_____
_____

# A Game of Catch

## ACTIVITY 6

### (Birth to Three Years of Age)

### MATERIALS NEEDED:

- Ball

### DIRECTIONS/OPTIONS:

- Depending on the child's abilities, roll, toss, or hold a ball with the child.

### GROSS MOTOR:

- Have the child roll or throw and catch the ball. If he/she cannot do that, help him/her just to hold the ball with his/her hands.
- Roll the ball away from the child and have her/him use different forms of locomotion to move to the ball and roll it back to you.
- Have the child walk around the room with the ball. Have him/her dribble it like a soccer ball, keeping it under control and using only his/her feet.

### FINE MOTOR:

- **Pincer Grasp:** Collect balls that are various sizes and weights. Instruct the child to practice grasping the balls with one or both hands.
- Have the child roll the ball back and forth between his/her own hands or feet, keeping it under control. Talk about the difference in using a soft tap and a harder tap and how that changes the speed at which the ball moves. Have the child also practice bouncing the ball and keeping it under control, or tossing it in the air and catching it himself/herself.

### ORAL LANGUAGE:

- Talk about how you can play catch or fetch with a dog. Explain that you can throw a ball or a Frisbee to a dog and how most dogs will bring it back to you! Ask the child what types of games people play that use a ball.
- **Vocabulary:** Use words such as roll, throw, ball, fetch, catch, etc. when playing with the ball. Encourage the child to imitate you while performing the actions.

- Sing the song with the child, substituting different words for "dog." For example, the child can sing, "Oh where, oh where, has my little doll/ball/toy gone?" and then search for that item within the classroom.

- **Phonemic Awareness:** Have the child bounce the ball for each syllable/word they say. You may need to do this first as a model for the child.

## WRITTEN LANGUAGE:

- **Pre-Literacy:** Look through a book or magazine and search for pictures of puppies, or have the child "read" a book to a stuffed puppy. Talk about things such as reading a book from front to back, one page at a time, using pictures to figure out what is happening, etc.

- Use a ball that has either letters or numbers on it. Show the child the letters/numbers as it rolls.

## SOCIAL/PRAGMATIC:

- Talk with the child about how a dog would hold the ball using his mouth.

- Other topics of discussion: How do people hold things? Can you hold things using anything other than your hands (for example, can you pick things up with your feet or by using both of your elbows? etc.)

## COGNITIVE:

- **Visual Closure:** Partially obstruct the ball from view using a blanket or another object. Encourage the child to find the ball when it is covered by the blanket.

- **Problem-Solving:** Place the ball somewhere where the child will need to develop a plan to retrieve it: for example, on the couch, in the toy box, etc.

## SENSORY:

- Have the child listen as the ball bounces on the floor. Bounce the ball very fast and very slow, roll the ball, or catch the ball. Do these different actions sound different?

- **Tactile Exploration:** Place several items of various textures in a box. Have the child close his or her eyes and try to identify the ball within the box. Or, you can rub different items of different textures on the child's hand/arm and talk about how they feel (soft, smooth, sticky, cold, warm, etc.)

# APPENDIX · Literacy in Children with Special Needs

Children with special needs many times present unique challenges for parents and service providers within the arena of literacy. What are those challenges and does the literature support the views that parents and providers may have? A brief discussion of the current literature relating to literacy and specific disabilities is included here.

## LITERACY DEVELOPMENT AND CHILDREN WITH COGNITIVE DISABILITIES

- It was previously assumed that a minimal IQ was mandatory to develop literacy, however new advances in writing research indicate that other skills (for example, phonemic awareness, print awareness, and vocabulary) and components are as vital for achieving some level of literacy (Browder, Gibbs, Ahlgrim-Delzell, Courtade, Mraz, and Flowers, 2009).

- Many parents of children with intellectual disabilities do not know what to expect in regard to literacy development for their child and may in fact have lower expectations for their child (van der Schuit, Peeter, Segers, van Balkon, and Verhoeven, 2009).

- Many children with intellectual disabilities will begin formal schooling with fewer emergent literacy skills than their typically developing peers (van Bysterveldt, Gillon, Foster-Cohen, 2010).

- Children with all levels of developmental and cognitive abilities benefit from being read to daily with support as needed to actively participate and engage with the text. (Browder, Gibbs, Ahlgrim-Delzell, Courtade, Mraz, and Flowers, 2009). For example, inclusion of movement depicted in the literacy prompt, manipulatives, repetition of vocabulary, use of sign language, assistance in book handling and manipulation, and assistive technology.

- Children with moderate and severe cognitive disabilities can learn phonics through systematic methods and literacy programs (Scruggs, 2008).

- Children with mild to moderate cognitive deficits can greatly benefit from a systematic and multi-level reading program (Hendrick, Katims, Carr, 1999), specifically, a program that has a balance between traditional and all-inclusive features.

- Hendrick, Katims, and Carr (1999) postulate that "Programs for students with mild to moderate mental retardation can be designed from pre-kindergarten to transition into the adult world in a way that balances necessary social skills/daily living skills with intensive and extensive literacy instruction" (p. 237).

- When children with intellectual disabilities acquire the foundational literacy skills considered to be prerequisites to reading, they may benefit more from the formal instruction received in the classroom (van Bysterveldt, Gillon, Foster-Cohen, 2008).

## LITERACY DEVELOPMENT IN CHILDREN WITH AUTISM SPECTRUM DISORDER

- "Little is known about the emergent literacy skills, print motivation, or home literacy environments of young children with ASD" (Lanter, Watson, Erickson, and Freeman, 2012).

- "Despite the fact that many individuals with autism are able to demonstrate skills that are directly related to literacy, such as print awareness and the ability to recognize common sight words, they are often seen as "too cognitively impaired" or "not ready for" instruction in this important area" (Mirenda, 2003).

- Research shows that opportunities for literacy and development of literacy skills help some children with ASD to develop oral language (Lanter and Watson, 2008).

- Children with ASD may experience difficulty understanding the function of literacy. Literacy intervention should be provided within natural contexts (Lanter and Watson, 2008).

- Although children with ASD exhibit inconsistent levels of achievement in literacy, many are responsive to emergent literacy intervention (Koppenhaver and Erickson, 2003).

- Children with ASD show a unique pattern as it relates to their interest in print and this appears related to later reading achievement (Frijter, Barron, & Brunello, 2000), specifically, they exhibit a high print interest.

- "For frequency of storybook reading, caregivers of children with ASD were found to engage in significantly less shared book reading in the home than their peers." (Dynia, Lawton, Logan, and Justice, 2014).

- "It is increasingly clear that most–if not all–students with autism can benefit from literacy instruction that incorporates the use of multiple instructional strategies that are carefully matched to the stages or phases of development through which all readers pass on their way from emergent reading to skilled reading." (Mirenda, 2003).

# Literacy Development in Children with Communication Impairments

- Children with communication impairments are at-risk for reading disabilities.

- It is recommended that parents and therapists provide increased shared book reading opportunities to children with communication impairment (Scheule, 2004).

- Children with communication impairments may demonstrate low levels of literacy engagement during shared reading activities that decrease the long-term literacy benefits of the activity (Kadervek, Pentimonti, and Justice, 2014).

- Research indicates that adult-child interactions can be negatively impacted by the presence of the child's communication impairment (Rabidoux and MacDonald, 2000).

- There is an increasing need for training and support for caregivers and early intervention providers to more effectively utilize shared book-reading practices (Kaderavek, Pentimonti, and Justice, 2014).

- At a group level, reading scores are generally depressed in children with a history of impaired language (Ricketts, 2011).

- Children at risk for communication impairment begin school with lower than average levels of vocabulary knowledge (Petrill, Logan, Sawyer, and Justice, 2014).

- Proactive training and engagement are needed to encourage and train parents to not only facilitate their child's acquisition of oral language but also their emergent literacy skills (Ezell, Justice, and Parsons, 2000).

# Literacy Development in Children with Hearing Impairment

- Most researchers agree that many children who are deaf or hearing impaired are at risk for significant reading defects, ultimately affecting their academic success and employment outcomes. It is important to note, however, that "Hearing loss in and of itself does not preclude the development of vocabulary, but it does impose constraints that educators must help students overcome" (Easterbrooks, Lederberg, Miller, Bergeron, and Connor, 2008).

- Research shows that for young deaf children, success in reading and academics in general may be facilitated by an early language environment, including exposure to visual language (Allen, Letteri, Choi and Dang, 2014). Specifically, studies of the brain have shown that children who use ASL as their primary language demonstrate the same trajectory for visual phonology as hearing children do for sound-based phonology (Petitto, 2000; Petitto, Katerelos, Levy, Gauna, Tetreault and Ferraro, 2001).

- Early exposure to a visual language greatly increases the likelihood that a deaf child will develop an array of cognitive, language, literacy, and social skills that will ultimately lead to higher levels of academic achievement. (Allen, Letterir, Choi and Dang, 2014).

- Parents and early intervention providers must understand that language and literacy development is a reciprocal relationship. Reading and writing skills must be prioritized in the same way as interaction and communication skills in order to provide a conducive environment for the development of these skills. (Stobbat and Alant, 2008).

- More emphasis is needed on the early acquisition of literacy skills and the specific role that parents have to play in engaging and meaningful text-based interactions with their children in a literacy-rich environment with high expectations for literacy development. (Stobbat and Alant, 2008).

- Children who are deaf or hard of hearing and were placed in literacy-rich environments were more likely to exhibit growth in rhyming. (Easterbrooks, Lederberg, and Connor, 2010).

- Children who are deaf or hearing impaired "are in need of multiple innovative reading instructional techniques aimed at creating opportunities for them to read, enjoy, and discuss connected English discourse." (Andrews, 2012).

- Research shows that "interactive story book reading supports deaf children's self-confidence as emergent readers, their comprehension, interest, and engagement with books, and their storytelling and word recognition skills." (Williams, 2004).

## LITERACY DEVELOPMENT IN CHILDREN WITH VISION IMPAIRMENT

- Children with visual impairment have limited access to incidental learning opportunities in the everyday environment. These children require the opportunity to experience the world in many different ways in order to comprehend and process these events. (Roe, Rogers, Donaldson, Gordon, and Meager, 2014).

- Changing the environment to increase movement and exploration at an earlier age will enhance all aspects of a child's development, including emergent literacy." (Stratton, 1996).

- Many children with visual impairments experience deficits with oral language including listening, attention, and concept development. (Stratton, 1996).

- The first 50 words that children with visual impairment typically acquire most likely will refer to the "here and now" (people, food, routines). (Roe, Rogers, Donaldson, Gordon, and Meager, 2014).

- Children with visual impairments require increased description of their environment, not just labeling. (Anderson, Dunlea, and Kekelis, 1993). Providing detailed and accurate descriptions of the people, objects, behaviors, and actions within the child's daily environment can have a positive effect on oral language development. (Erickson and Hatton, 2007).

To develop early stages of literacy through braille, children need to develop language skills, early book skills, and understanding of the world to ensure comprehension but they also need to develop tactile skills including tactile discrimination of braille letters. (Roe, Rogers, Donaldson, Gordon and Meager, 2014).

# References

For your convenience, you may download a PDF version of the posters and templates in this book from our dedicated website: www.pesi.com/Thatcher

Allen, T.E., Letteri, A., Choi, S.H., & Dang, D. (2014). Early visual language exposure and emergent literacy in preschool deaf children: Findings from a national longitudinal study. *American Annals of the Deaf*, 4, 346-358.

Anderson, E.S., Dunlea, A., & Kekelis, L.S. (1984). Blind children's language: Resolving some differences. *Journal of Child Language*, 11, 645-664.

Andrews, J.F. (2012). Reading to deaf children who sign: A response to Williams (2012) and suggestions for future research. *American Annals of the Deaf*, 157(3), 307-319.

Browder, D., Gibbs, S., Ahlgrim-Delzell, G.R., Mraz, M., & Flowers, C. (2009). Literacy for students with severe developmental disabilities. What should we teach and what should we hope to achieve? *Remedial and Special Education*, 30(5), 269-282.

Catts, H.W. (1993). The relationship between speech-language impairments and reading disabilities. *Journal of Speech and Hearing Review*, 36, 948-958.

Dickinson, D. K., & McCabe, A. (2001). Bringing It All Together: The Multiple Origins, Skills, and Environmental Supports of Early Literacy. *Learning Disabilities Research & Practice*, 16(4), 186-202.

Duursma, E. (2014). The Effects of Fathers' and Mothers' Reading to Their Children on Language Outcomes of Children Participating in Early Head Start in the United States. *Fathering*, 12(3), 283-302.

Dynia, J.M., Lawton, K., Logan, J.A., Justice, L.M. (2014). Comparing emergent-literacy skills and home-literacy environment of children with autism and their peers. *Topics in Early Childhood Special Education*, 34(3), 142-153.

Easterbrooks, S.R., Lederberg, A.R., Miller, E.M., Bergeron, J.P., & Connor, C. (2008). Emergent literacy skills during early childhood in children with hearing loss: Strengths and weaknesses. *The Volta Review*, 2, 91-114.

Easterbooks, S.R., Lederberg, A.R., & Connor, C.M. (2010). Contributions of the emergent literacy environment to literacy outcomes for young children who are deaf. *American Annals of the Deaf*, 155(4), 467-480.

Erickson, K.A. & Hatton, D. (2007). Expanding understanding of emergent literacy: Empirical support for a new framework. *Journal of Visual Impairment & Blindness*, 101(5), 261-277.

Ezell, H.K., Justice, L.M., & Parsons, D. (2000). Enhancing the emergent literacy skills of pre-schoolers with communication disorders: a pilot investigation. *Child Language Teaching and Therapy*, 16(2), 121-140.

Frijters, J.C., Barron, R.W., & Brunello, M. (2000). Direct and mediated influences of literary and literacy interest on prereaders' oral vocabulary and early written language skill. *Journal of Educational Psychology*, 92, 466-477.

Froiland, J. M., Powell, D. R., Diamond, K. E., & Seung-Hee, C. S. (2013). Neighborhood Socioeconomic Well-Being, Home Literacy, and Early Literacy Skills of At-Risk Preschoolers. *Psychology in the Schools*, 50(8), 755-769.

Goldstein, H. (2011). Knowing what to teach provides a roadmap for early literacy intervention. *Journal of Early Intervention*, 33(4), 268-280.

Hart, B. & Risley, T. (1995). *Meaningful differences in the everyday lives of American children*. Baltimore, MD: Brookes Publishing.

Hendrick, W.B., Katims, D.S., & Carr, N.J. (1999). Implementing a multimethod, multilevel literacy program for students with mental retardation. *Focus on Autism and Other Developmental Disabilities*, 14(4), 231-239.

International Reading Association and National Association of Young Children. (1998). Learning to read and write: Developmentally appropriate practices for young children. A joint position statement of the International Reading Association (IRA) and the National Association for the Education of Young Children (NAEYC), adopted 1998. *Young Children*, 53(4), 3-46.

Johnston, S.S., McDonnel, A.P., & Hawken, L.S. (2008). Enhancing outcomes in early literacy for young children with disabilities: Strategies for success. *Intervention in School and Clinic*, 43(4), 210-217.

Kaderavek, J.N., Pentimonti, J.M., & Justice, L.M. (2014). Children with communication impairments: Caregivers' and teachers' shared book-reading quality and children's level of engagement. *Child Language Teaching and Therapy*, 30(3), 289-302.

Kirk, S.M., Coleman, R.V., Looney, E.C., & Kirk, E.P. (2014). Using physical activity to teach academic content: A study of the effects on literacy in Head Start preschoolers. *Early Childhood Education Journal*, 42, 181-189.

Koppenhaver, D.A. & Erickson, K.A. (2003). Natural emergent literacy supports for preschoolers with autism and severe communication impairments. *Topics in Language Disorders*, 23(4), 283-292.

Koppenhaver, D.A., Pierce, P.L., & Yoder, D.E. (1995). AAC, FC, and the ABC's: Issues and relationships. *American Journal of Speech Language Pathology*, 4, 5-14.

Lanter, E. & Watson, L.R. (2008). Promoting literacy in students with ASD: The basics for the SLP. *Language, Speech, and Hearing Services in Schools*, 39, 33-43.

McDonnell, A.P., Hawken, L.S., Johnston, S.S., Kidder, J.E., Lynes, M.J., & McDonnell, J.J. (2014). Emergent literacy practices and support for children with disabilities: A national survey. *Education and Treatment of Children*, 37(3), 495-530.

Mirenda, P. (2003). 'He's not really a reader.....": Perspectives on supporting literacy development in individuals with autism. *Topics in Language Disorders*, 23(4), 271-282.

National Association for the Education of Young Children. (2009). *Developmentally appropriate practice in early childhood programs serving children birth though age 8*. A position statement of the National Association for the Education of Young Children.

Petitto, L.A. (2000). On the biological foundations of human language. In H. Lane & K. Emmorey (Eds.). *The signs of language revisited: An anthology in honor of Ursula Bellugi and Edward Klima* (pp. 447-471). Mahwah, NJ: Erlbaum.

Petitto, L.A., Katerekos, M., Levy, B.G., Gauna, K., Tetreault, K., & Ferraro, V. (2001). Bilingual signed and spoken language acquisition from birth: Implications for the mechanisms underlying early bilingual language acquisition. *Journal of Child Language*, 28(2), 453-496.

Petrill, S.A., Logan, J.A., Sawyer, B.E., & Justice, L.M. (2014). It depends: Conditional correlation between frequency of storybook reading and emergent literacy skills in children with language impairments. *Journal of Learning Disabilities*, 47(6), 491-502.

Rabidoux, P. & MacDonald, J. (2000). An interactive taxonomy of mothers and children during storybook interactions. *American Journal of Speech Language Pathology*, 9, 331-44.

Ricketts, J. (2011). Research review: Reading comprehension in developmental disorders of language and communication. *The Journal of Child Psychology and Psychiatry*, 52(11), 1111-1123.

Roe, J., Rogers, S., Donaldson, M., Gordon, C., & Meager, N. (2014). Teaching literacy through braille in mainstream settings whilst promoting inclusion: Reflections on our practice. *International Journal of Disability, Development, and Education*, 61(2), 165-177.

Scheffner Hammer, C., Farkas, G. & Maczuga, S. (2010). The Language and Literacy Development of Head Start Children: A Study Using the Family and Child Experiences Survey Database. *Language, Speech, and Hearing Services in Schools*, 41, 70-83.

Schuele, C. (2004). The impact of developmental speech and language impairments on the acquisition of literacy skills. *Mental Retardation and Developmental Disabilities Research Reviews*, 10, 176-83.

Scruggs, A. (2008). Effective reading instruction strategies for students with significant cognitive disabilities. *Electronic Journal for Inclusive Education*, 2(3).

Stobbart, C. & Alant, E. (2008). Home-based literacy experiences of severely to profoundly deaf preschoolers and their hearing parents. *Journal of Developmental and Physical Disabilities*, 20, 139-153.

Stratton, J.M. (1996). Emergent literacy: A new perspective. *Journal of Visual Impairment & Blindness*, 90(3), 177-183.

Thatcher, K. & McVicker, C. (2005). Literacy into therapy: The first steps provider. *Indiana First Steps Newsletter*. May/June, 2005, Vol. 1.

Tomporowski, P.D., Davis, C.L., Miller, P.H., & Naglieri, J.A. (2008). Exercise and children's intelligence, cognition, and academic achievement. *Educational Psychology Review*, 20, 111-131.

Van Bysterveldt, A., Gillon, G., & Foster-Cohen, S. (2010). Literacy environments for children with Down syndrome: What's happening at home? *Down Syndrome Research and Practice*, 12(2), 98-102.

Van Der Schuit, M., Peeters, M., Segers, E., Van Balkom, H., & Verhoeven, L. (2009). Home literacy environment of pre-school children with intellectual disabilities. *Journal of Intellectual Disability Research*, 53, 1024-1037.

Williams, C. (2004). Emergent literacy of deaf children. *Journal of Deaf Studies and Deaf Education*, 9(4), 352-365.